C000060863

Sonic Branding

Sonn Burging

SONIC BRANDING

AN INTRODUCTION

Daniel M. Jackson

edited by

Paul Fulberg

palgrave
macmillan

© Daniel M. Jackson and Paul Fulberg 2003
Foreword © Fru Hazlitt 2003

All rights reserved. No reproduction, copy or transmission of this
publication may be made without written permission.

No paragraph of this publication may be reproduced, copied or transmitted
save with written permission or in accordance with the provisions of the
Copyright, Designs and Patents Act 1988, or under the terms of any licence
permitting limited copying issued by the Copyright Licensing Agency, 90
Tottenham Court Road, London W1T 4LP.

Any person who does any unauthorized act in relation to this publication
may be liable to criminal prosecution and civil claims for damages.

The authors have asserted their rights to be identified
as the authors of this work in accordance with the Copyright,
Designs and Patents Act 1988.

First published 2003 by
PALGRAVE MACMILLAN
Houndmills, Basingstoke, Hampshire RG21 6XS and
175 Fifth Avenue, New York, N.Y. 10010
Companies and representatives throughout the world

PALGRAVE MACMILLAN is the global academic imprint of the Palgrave
Macmillan division of St. Martin's Press, LLC and of Palgrave Macmillan Ltd.
Macmillan® is a registered trademark in the United States, United Kingdom
and other countries. Palgrave is a registered trademark in the European
Union and other countries.

ISBN 1–4039–0519–3   hardback
ISBN 978-1-403-90519-2 hardback

This book is printed on paper suitable for recycling and made from fully
managed and sustained forest sources. Logging, pulping and manufacturing
processes are expected to conform to the environmental regulations of the
country of origin.

A catalogue record for this book is available from the British Library.

Library of Congress Cataloging-in-Publication Data
Jackson, Daniel M., 1972-
    Sonic branding : an introduction / by Daniel M. Jackson and
edited by Paul Fulberg.
    p. cm.
    Includes bibliographical references and index.
    ISBN 1–4039–0519–3 (cloth)
      1. Advertising—Brand name products. 2. Music in advertising.
I. Fulberg, Paul, 1973–II. Title
HF6161.B4J3 2003
659.14—dc21   2003046970

Printed and bound in Great Britain by
CPI Antony Rowe, Chippenham and Eastbourne

Contents

Contents

List of figures

List of tables

Foreword

I have a *dream* today ...

If there is one talent I have always wished to possess, it is very definitely the ability to sing or at the very least the ability to write things that other people could sing. For most of us music has a unique and often disturbing power and those who can wield it are fortunate indeed.

Speaking for myself, I know that after a bad start to my day, good humour can be magically restored by the rendition on the radio of one of my favourite Abba tunes. Of course I may well be alone in my choice of tune but believe that the general principle applies to most of us. Music moves us from one emotion to another, usually without us even realizing when or especially how it happens. For those of us who lack the singer's talents, it is worth noting that music is not alone in its ability. There is another gift possessed of few that can evoke a similar and in some cases even more extraordinary response from an audience; the talent of the orator.

I do hope I will cause no offence if I say that neither Adolph Hitler nor Winston Churchill were in a 'Hollywood' sense attractive men but it is clear that when they spoke to the masses, the masses were moved in an awesome and often alarming manner. With so little to offer visually, it has always interested me as I listened to recordings from the time, that the key to the emotive power of the men's speeches was not what they were saying but how they were saying it. I ask you right now to read aloud the following immortal words, spoken by Churchill with regard to the Battle of Britain: 'Never in the field of human conflict, was so much owed by so many to so few.' You may sound OK and you may think as you read that this was a fine and well-constructed thing to say. Listen, however, to the original recordings of that same speech. Let Winston himself speak the words and I defy anyone not to experience even the smallest of shivers. Perhaps this is why history remembers the orator and forgets the speech-writer. Did Martin Luther King write those immortal words himself? And if he did not, who cares! The passion with which he spoke them is what stays in the memory; his tone of voice summing up everything for which he stood. The point I am making is that the emotive power of sound should never be overlooked or underestimated when just a song or a few words, presented in the right way, can move so many people.

I spent some years working for a large group of radio stations in the UK and spent many an hour extolling the virtues of radio as an advertising medium. At the time the power of radio was rarely understood by advertisers in the UK, though audiences had appreciated it for decades. It suffered a poor image with ad agencies, particularly when it had to compete with the more glamorous world of television commercials with big budgets and big fees. To convince people, we had to be creative and would think nothing of putting a bunch of potential advertisers into a darkened room, asking them to shut their eyes and emploring them to understand the power of sound and its ability to appeal to the imagination. This took about a minute ... just long enough to hear Churchill singing 'Dancing Queen'.

The truth was and still is that making a successful radio commercial is considerably more difficult than making a successful television commercial. It is even more challenging in relation to making press or poster ads. Sound is a very delicate, ephemeral, ethereal medium. This makes the line between creative success and failure very thin and where the right words, tone or music can evoke the most powerful of responses, the wrong words or the wrong tone can very quickly irritate and even result in damage to the perception of the brand. Laurence Olivier can make sense of Shakespeare's words for us in a way that 99% of people cannot. In the same way, no one can make of 'Bohemian Rhapsody' what the immortal voice of Freddie Mercury achieved. These examples show us that conveying the true emotions of a message or indeed a brand is an interpretive art that requires talent, training and experience.

Of course, we can learn from the masters and in the UK I would rate Hamlet Cigars as having the best, most recognizable, most evocative sonic branding. Tobacco advertising regulations have restricted them to radio for some years but their use of Bach's 'Air on the G String' has enabled them to connect emotionally just as effectively as TV would have allowed. After 40 years of consistent use, Bach's piece was so well established that ads only needed to play three or four seconds of it to connect with their audience. In that way they have developed a sonic logo like Intel's or Yahoo!'s. By having this, they get the freedom to say whatever they like in whatever tone is desired for a campaign, whilst still generating instant recognition.

Sonic logos like Yahoo!'s and the corresponding 'Do you Yahoo!' have worked so well because they truly are a part of the branding of the company and the audience hears them as consistent with the values. This is the real art and the reason why time, care and attention should be invested in sonic branding. If it is done correctly, all the brand's values can be conveyed in just a few seconds. Another fantastic UK example of this is the brilliant Carphone Warehouse, a company that built its brand on the power of sound and sonic branding and became a market leader without spending a penny on pictures! Its sonic branding started as a whistled jingle and evolved into the long term licensing of a track called 'Connected' by the Stereo MCs. Both became strong brand properties because they used music and words in the right way to convey the emotions of the brand and they did it consistently.

And finally, radio is the spiritual home of sonic branding but today, as brand owners, we have access to a range of media where sound can be used to brand. As a nervous but very frequent flyer, I have come to love one brand's sonics more than any other. British Airways have used 'that tune' (Delibe's 'Flower Duet' from *Lakmé*) in all their ads and on the phone for years but the place it means the most to me is when it is played on the planes. It calms and soothes but most importantly for the jetlagged, it is one final reassurance that one is indeed on the right plane, headed for home rather than darkest Peru.

In conclusion then, let me leave you with this. If you care about what your brand looks like then you should most certainly care what it sounds like. If you get that bit right then the responses you evoke will be powerful indeed. And if you are about to make that speech or write that commercial then don't forget that tone and presentation are everything. The reward for getting these right is a freedom of expression you may dream about; the licence to say anything you like. After all, as the politicians will tell you 'a true diplomat is a person who can tell you to go to hell in such a way that you already look forward to the trip!'

FRU HAZLITT
Managing Director
UK Yahoo!

Preface

Be yourself. Be honest and express how you feel. Listen to how others feel, empathize and try to give them what they want and need. Treat everybody in this way, every time you meet them. Make an effort and think it through.

This is my mantra and it helps remind me who I am. This in turn helps me evaluate the situations presented to me every day as a businessman and brand practitioner. Whenever ideas are presented to me or I present ideas to others, I try to remind myself of how I should be and it helps me through. In my opinion, everyone needs a mantra but then as someone once prosaically said 'opinions are like arseholes, everybody's got one'.

Undeniably, this book is full of opinions. In an industry as young as branding and sonic branding, where quantitative analysis is in its infancy and success is hard to define, there is not much else to go on. I'll say that again before moving on. Branding is a new industry. Though it draws upon the human experience of many thousands of years and many different disciplines and beliefs, the industry dedicated to the creation and management of brands is really just 50 or so years old.

Sonic branding has its unconscious routes in the ancient songs of our pre-historic ancestors but it has existed as a recognized business discipline for just a couple of decades and has only taken on its current levels of sophistication in the last few years. So, we are in the realm of the new and in such realms, we seek the opinions of the wise to guide us. Together with Paul Fulberg, who has edited this book and Ali Johnson, Creative Director of Sonicbrand, I have immersed myself in the subject of sonic branding since I gave up my day job to found the United Kingdom's first sonic branding specialist in 1999.

The wise people, whose opinions I sought out and listened to when founding the company were the experts in the varying and disparate fields of study and commerce that made up the then fragmented sonic branding world. The skills and knowledge that are required to practice sonic branding have existed for some time but never, it seems, in one place; so, by hearing the opinions of those working in film composition, musical theatre, advertising, branding and design, to name a few, Sonicbrand started to bring together a new specialism and form the cogent arguments that support it.

Though it was never an intention or goal to write a book, Sonicbrand did set out to become the first experts in the discipline. In that respect we now feel qualified to give our 'expert' opinions on the subject. Billy Connolly says: 'Beware people who claim they know the answers ... keep the company of people who are trying to understand the question.'[1] We have not sought to give all the answers in this book because we do not have them ourselves. We have sought, however, to ask all the important questions. Creative processes are driven by questions; what to include and what to leave out. Sonic branding is no different and perhaps brings the need for questioning into sharper relief than many other fields of creativity. Music, the bedrock of sonic branding, is a universally understood language and this leaves no room for dogmatic assertions. If it is not right, everybody knows.

Peter Drucker wrote in his excellent book *Post Capitalist Society*, that 'knowledge is the only meaningful resource today'.[2] I believe this to be true and in seeking the knowledge that I have committed to paper in this book, I have tried to ask as many questions as I could, in an effort to test and retest Sonicbrand's theories and quantify our experiences. This has been an invaluable process with benefits for my business and for me as a person.

Paul and I have questioned many of the leading brand experts working today on all sides of the business. We have found a mixed bag of opinions, most of them expert. This undoubtedly helped us improve our knowledge of what brands are and what branding means. It also proved to be great fun and started valuable dialogue between Sonicbrand and many other businesses. Transcripts of the conversations with the experts are included in the appendix to this book as a primary source for your reference and I can thoroughly recommend writing a book as a way of meeting and talking to new people.

My other major research involved spending a lot of time reading what has already been written about branding, brands and to a far lesser extent, sonic branding. Though this area of our research has been less rewarding than the face to face stuff, it has provided me with some much needed points of reference for this, the first book about sonic branding.

The reason for referencing existing brand theories is that sonic branding is a logical next step in the disciplines of branding, the principles of which have been around for some time but are constantly evolving. This book builds upon the understanding that has already been committed to paper and seeks, broadly, to do two 'new' things for anyone who reads it. First, we want to give you the most up to date and useful definitions of brand and branding. These will serve as a basis for the sonic branding process and allow us to show where and how sonics fit in to the existing 'brandscape'. Second, we want to let you know why sonic branding is potentially the most powerfully emotive and expressive weapon in the brand armoury.

Furthermore, we want to share our processes and thoughts regarding the creation and management of sonic branding, empowering you to take an active role in sonics for brands.

Sonic branding is such a far-reaching discipline, that we have had to write this book with an incredibly diverse audience in mind. Board level executives, managers, marketeers, advertising creatives, advertising planners, composers, musicians, radio salesmen, TV producers, film directors, students of media and communications, entrepreneurs, City analysts, anti-capitalist conspiracy theorists and just about anyone else who wants to know why that Intel thingy is so catchy, should get something out of this book. No matter what your interest in the subject, by the end of reading it, I hope you feel you have gained a new perspective on the worlds of brands and sound. I also hope you take this perspective and start to question it and us, thereby helping to evolve the collective understanding of how brands communicate through sound. At Sonicbrand, our passions for this business fuel our desire to talk about it and write about it. It is this passion that has seen our business grow from a belief in 1998 to its successful and respected position today.

It is rare to be able to turn a hobby into a living but that is what sonic branding has given to all of us at Sonicbrand. What was once my party trick; being able to recall almost any jingle, musical ad campaign or TV theme tune has become a valuable commercial skill. The music that corporations have created over the years has become a valuable part of our culture and the desire to tap into the strength of feelings and memory that this music creates drives the sonic branding industry today. A number of historical strands weave together in the history of sonic branding both creatively and on an industry level. The great thing about history is that everyone has their own perspective on events but as far as I'm concerned, this is how it all started.

Le marque sonique

The term 'marque sonique' was first coined, as far as we know, in the mid-1980s by French commercial radio guru Jean Pierre Baçelon. As a radio producer turned airtime salesman, he has been credited with identifying the benefits of sonic branding on radio. His practice of archiving, analysing and categorizing radio commercials led him to the conclusions that radio advertising containing sonic branding elements achieved greater success in awareness, sales and repeat business for commercial radio stations. Through his role as Directeur du développement radio at IP France, the commercial radio group, he spread the word of his findings around Europe, setting up radio archives, stylishly termed 'laboratories' for his employer.

Between 1989 and 1992 investments by IP France in Capital Radio Group lead to Jean Pierre working closely with Diarmid Moncrieff of Media Sales and Marketing UK (now Capital Radio Sales). Together, they created the first English translations of his ideas and beliefs under the heading 'sonic branding'. Diarmid's evangelical, maverick style of presentation has spread the gospel of sonic branding in the United Kingdom over the last ten years. His primary purpose for talking about the subject was similar to Baçelon's; sonic branding aids the selling of radio airtime. Essentially the pitch has been to turn clients on to the medium of radio by proving to them that sound is a powerful and viable brand communications tool.

The sonic branding sell, as further adopted by Andrew Ingram at the Radio Advertising Bureau UK (RAB), has helped convince many advertisers to try radio and has seen the medium grow from holding a 2% share of display advertising budgets in 1992 to a 7% share in 2002. It was during my time working with both Diarmid and Andrew at Capital Radio plc (1997–9) that I became convinced that sonic branding was (and is) a subject worthy of greater study and with far wider implications than just as a radio airtime sales tool.

My time at Capital coincided with a period of enormous growth in Internet, mobile telephony, interactive TV and audio-enabled consumer products. The bubble was inflating rapidly and it seemed like every new idea was going to revolutionize the way people acted and the way they could be marketed to. It was also a time of great optimism in the advertising and branding industries as the Dotcoms threw their backers' cash around with abandon and new ideas were welcomed with open cheque books. The new technologies were heralded as media platforms capable of delivering richly creative messages to consumers. Importantly for me, every new platform had sound delivery built in and created a whole new realm for sonic branding that added to the need for brands to have some way to express themselves in sound.

The bubble burst but the revolution that started then is still happening today. Almost all brands now own multimedia empires that range from print to Internet, TV, radio, mobile and retail. This means that brands now face challenges previously only applicable to the biggest businesses and broadcasters: they have to brand a number of different media channels.

Back in the bubble, those in charge of what could loosely be termed sonic branding in the UK at the end of the last century were advertising agencies. The focus for the ad business at the time was high-impact advertising, with seemingly little thought given to longevity of planning or campaigns.

Ironically, in the name of brand building, music in ads became hijacked by a kind of musical licensing ego trip. Microsoft had the Rolling Stones, Apple got Elvis and Nortel bagged The Beatles. In their wake, the smaller brands grabbed whatever they could afford from the shelves of the record store. Though this strategy did have impact, it left most brands with nowhere to go. Licensing big tracks costs big money and it proved an unsustainable activity for everyone, even mighty Microsoft.

The inconsistency and lack of thought of ad agencies created the opportunity for a specialist approach to sonic branding to take hold. It was obvious from the lack of a strategic approach in the agency world that the basic principles of branding – differentiation and consistency – were being ignored in the selection of music for brands. As well as the relatively memorable and successful Windows 98 'Start Me Up' and iMac 'Blue Suede Shoes' campaigns, there were disastrous wastes of money and effort that helped us identify who was going wrong and how. For example, the reputed £1 million paid by Vauxhall Motors through their agency, Lowes, for the latest track by The Verve, 'Bitter Sweet Symphony'.

One of the biggest car launch campaigns ever used a string sample taken from a Rolling Stones track that had been used by The Verve. Musically, it was intelligent but downbeat. Its classical nature was dramatic and at odds with the modest, family oriented personality of the Vauxhall Astra. The music simply did not hit the marque. It ran on TV and radio ads for less than a year and then the licence ran out. No more licence meant no more track. A brand property that was arguably wrong in the first place, had cost £1 million to buy and had many times that amount spent on advertising it, was no longer a brand property at all. Furthermore, the Astra failed to make the number one slot in the car market and the model and marque has suffered through its inconsistent branding ever since. In the last year or so, it has been widely reported that Lowes has lost its long-held grip on the Vauxhall advertising account. The beneficiary seems to have been London agency Delaney Lund Knox Warren (DLKW). Interestingly, DLKW is an agency that has made much of its reputation by finding a creative way to put music at the long-term heart of campaigns for the Halifax, a retail bank.

Back in the spring of 1999, when Lowes was spending Vauxhall's money, I was working with clients from the motoring sector, targeting them specifically with sonic presentations. I was fortunate enough to have a chance to work with one of the ad men I really respected. Paul Fulberg was an account director at Creative Strategy, an offshoot of Grey UK that was later to be merged with its parent company. We first met at University and kept in touch as our careers took off in London. We had already run a successful campaign for his client, Smint, on Capital and he was open to some new ideas for one of his other clients, Skoda Auto. In examining sonic branding for Skoda, Paul became convinced that this really was a good idea and was amazed as I was that nobody else was out there doing it.

We founded the company in November 1999. The following year, Ali Johnson joined us as our creative director, bringing his extensive knowledge and experience of working with music in the collaborative environment of music theatre. When we started out we set ourselves the goal of demystifying sound and educating our clients so that they could collaborate with us. Our desire is still to wake up our clients to the amazing opportunities of sonic branding and to work with them on the extremely rewarding and enjoyable projects that result.

One of the greatest and most challenging aspects of sonic branding is the enormous subjectivity that surrounds the issue of music and brands. The creative processes we have developed, which we will explain in later sections, have been designed to find a path through this subjectivity. Similarly, we have always taken the time to define our terms in order to minimize the subjectivity of our language. In this way we have built our success based upon honesty, understanding and delivery of strategic and creative solutions that meet expectations, in a field where nobody, until now, had really known what to expect. Our clients, of course, have played a massive role in our growth. It takes a certain bravery to be the first to invest in new ideas and we have been lucky enough to have worked with some brave and intelligent people. The fact that sonic branding is now a budget line on so many marketing plans is a testament to how far our clients have enabled us to go.

The sonic branding industry as a whole has also grown and continues to do so throughout the current and ongoing recession. We think this is another pretty good indicator of the validity of the idea. This together with the reactions of almost every person we have talked to about sonic branding has led us to believe that there is genuine value in the subject. Sonic branding is a hot topic and it is more than hot air. The interest and investment has come about because some of the most interesting and successful corporate and consumer brands out there practise some sort of sonic branding and have been doing so for many years. Sonic branding is not a fad or the latest thing, it is a codification of disparate but long-established business practices.

The success of companies like Intel, Starbucks and BMW (GB) have provided us with some incredibly compelling case studies that give real-world demonstrations of how great brands have been taking at least some advantage of the power of sound for many years. Despite this, the vast majority of brands own no sonic branding and have given it very little thought. This makes sonic branding one of the great communications opportunities today because putting some thought into all communications is not only desirable but absolutely necessary for long-term effective and efficient brand building. Brand building is what it is all about, essentially creating and communicating the long-term benefits of brands for their stakeholders. To help define what this entails, I have called upon many of the leading brand experts in this country to define brands, branding and some of the other phrases that are bandied around these days.

A lifetime as a consumer and a career in advertising and media has exposed me to plenty of thinking on all kinds of brands but it was not until I started researching this book that I found any number of branding experts who could agree on what is the essence of a brand. Thankfully, I eventually found a large enough consensus for me to be reasonably sure that this book subscribes to the latest and broadest beliefs about brands. Confusingly, many brand experts, expressive people all, were unable to give succinct explanations of brands and even those who agreed on what defines a brand used the different words to do so. To ease my furrowed brow I turned to the most obvious places for definitions, starting with the two dictionaries that I own. Both have failed to give me definitions that related to the real world and though I love the clarity of dictionary definitions and always use them as a starting point for constructing arguments, they have been of relatively little value here.

Perhaps the most famous book about brands in the last five years was Naomi Klein's *No Logo*. So, I read it, looking for the detailed and credible brand definition that I thought would underpin her arguments. What I found was this, the only brand definition offered in Ms Klein's 500-page critique: 'Think of the brand as the core meaning of the modern corporation.'[3] Her book was a great success, launching the Naomi Klein brand to a world-wide constituency but her definition was simplistic and became the basis for millions of people's perceptions of brands.

This book subscribes to a different and more sophisticated definition of brands and, while the *No Logo* debate is a good one, we will not investigate it too much here. The fact that Klein is able to create her own definition of a brand and then use it as a basis for attacking them is testament enough to the issues that can arise when nobody agrees what anything means. The lack of a common lexicon has been a major challenge for this book and it remains a challenge for the ever-expanding branding industry. Transparency and clarity are vital for rebuilding the trust in brand investment that was dented by Dotcom excesses from clients and ad agencies. It is not coincidental that large businesses like Marks and Spencer and Boots, in the UK, have downgraded the marketing function to below board level in the last year. Trust, through plain talking, will have to be rebuilt before branding is elevated once again.

In order to follow my own advice and convey information about sonic branding clearly, I have included a glossary in this book. Part of my inspiration comes from the website of Landor Associates, the global brand and identity specialist. Landor has a very good branding glossary. It is clear and informative but unfortunately, nobody reads it or uses it, not even the majority of Landor staff! I hope that the terms as defined in these pages can become a common language for the industry, allowing clients to compare like with like when holding pitches.

If one considers a lack of common lexicon in branding to be an issue, then imagine for a moment the problems facing the infant sonic branding industry. Since Sonicbrand was founded, when Google™ threw up 20 'sonic branding' results, the phrase has become a bandwagon for any composer or digital designer who ever got a corporate commission. Flattering as this might be, the need to define what is and is not sonic branding has become paramount as the art and science are in danger of being devalued before they have really been perfected. We have no desire for Naomi Klein to write *No Sonic Logo* in the years to come.

In Part One we will examine sound from the many perspectives that relate to our subject, including music in film, music in advertising and sound as a medium. We will also examine the role of sound in our lives and its effects upon our minds and emotions. Part Two will delve more deeply into the subject of brands, seeking to convey the understanding of brands that has amassed over the last 2,000 years. We will examine what is good about brands and particularly, what positive impact they could have on the future. Brands, on all levels, are desirable because brands bring benefits. Branded goods and services generate wealth. They are popular and are more desirable than non-branded goods and services. Branded organizations have greater success than other organizations. Consider New Labour, the greatest brand in British political history. Through naming, symbols, colour, font and the consistent use of language, New Labour came to power. They were even involved in sonic branding, selecting and consistently using D-Ream's 'Things Can Only Get Better' as a campaign theme. By embracing the techniques of branding, New Labour was acknowledging and endorsing the realities of modern life: the majority of the people want brands with everything.

This is not a political book, however, despite the obvious links between brands and the capitalist democracy that supports them. This is a book about the relationship between brands, people and sound. We are at a point in the development of brands where it would be easy to condemn the whole system that creates them, just because a few companies have been found to betray the trust of their stakeholders. To do this would be as ludicrous as to condemn any religion on the basis of the actions of a few very misguided individuals.

Part Three will describe the processes and creativity required for exercising the art and science of sonic branding, before examining a number of the most important and useful case studies available. We have gathered together case studies to show how sonic branding is already out there and that those practising it are reaping rewards. When one looks at the brands involved, including eight of the top ten global brands as defined by Interbrand, it is clear that great brands have been taking at least some advantage of the power of sound for many years. My aim is to share the knowledge of what to do and how to do it. I hope you enjoy learning about this new and exciting discipline and that you reward the world with more and better sonic branding for years to come.

DANIEL M. JACKSON

Acknowledgements

The author would like to thank all those who contributed in their own way to this book, especially Oliver from Engine for his writing and Anna, Nick and Simon from Cyan London for their illustrations. Further thanks go to Stephen Rutt and Jacky Kippenberger of Palgrave Macmillan for their belief and hard work.

Paul contributed far more than an editor should and Ali provided great inside information. With their help, Sonicbrand continues to lead the industry. Special thanks to my sister, Caroline, and to my parents, Paul and Pamela Jackson, for their infinite knowledge and support. Finally, my greatest thanks to Sara, for her educated opinions and late-night pasta deliveries.

For my Granny

PART I

What is Sonic Branding?

There is nothing new under the sun but there are many things that go unnoticed. Sonic branding seemed like a new idea in the 1980s but its roots go back much further. The primordial value of music in our culture has meant that history is strewn with lessons that are of value to the discipline of sonic branding today. This is lucky, because our understanding of brands and how they interact with us is sophisticated enough for us to realize that sonic branding can mean many different things in many different scenarios.

There is a rich history of brands using music or sound in their communications. Similarly, there is a fantastic amount to be learned about how the dominant art-form of our age, the movie, has influenced what we hear and the way we hear it. Movie music has provided us with a common musical language. Thanks to the movies, for example, we all know that violins playing fast, high-pitched notes repeatedly rising (as in the shower scene of Hitchcock's *Psycho*) are very scary. Similarly, we know that a rising minor second interval (the smallest gap between two notes on a piano), bowed on a double bass, means that a shark attack is about to take place (John Williams, *Jaws*). Perhaps more importantly, the movie business, with its three-way creative relationships between writer, director and composer give sonic branding its working model. For us, the triumvirate of brand, client and sonic branding composer, are inter-related in very similar ways.

In this chapter, we will briefly examine the scope and nature of sonic branding, defining a few key terms as we go. We will then examine the parallel histories of the jingle, music in advertising and the Hollywood music industries as they form the foundations for the strategic and creative lessons of sonic branding. They are also areas of the culture where new technology has presented challenges and opportunities for communications, the solutions to which are applicable to almost all brands in the electronic age.

Imagine the scene – it is late May, the year is 1999 and two newly weds, are enjoying the last, precious few days of their honeymoon on the beautiful and largely unspoilt island of Capri. We are in the middle of the Mediterranean, some miles from mainland Italy. The industrial bustle of Naples and the tourist hustle of Pompeii are worlds away as the young couple take time to enjoy the first flushes of an everlasting relationship.

The scent of olive groves mixes with the smell of the sea and the aroma of the fresh double espresso with which they toast this particularly fine afternoon, sitting in a café, the walls of which are adorned by smiley-sun plates, so typical of Capri. Below the café, inescapable on such a small island, the gentle sounds of the sea can be heard as the water laps the shore, rushes through the handsome rocks of the coastline and moves the shingle of the beach with an assured rhythm and a relaxed power. This is quite a scene. The kind they promise in the brochures. The couple talk of plans for the future, conspiring to remain on the island and bask in the glow of this day forever, in this perfect place. The husband is lost in his wife's words and the world and all its beauty disappears. All he can see or hear is her.

And then, wrenched with the force of a supermarket mum grabbing the arm of her four-year-old pick'n'mix thief, I was back at work. Not physically but mentally. It was head-turning and unmistakable. I had not even been listening so it came as some surprise to me that now, rather than hearing the sweet nothings of my love, I was listening to a radio commercial ad for, I assume, computers. You see, I speak very little Italian. That is why my brain had decided not to listen to the radio station that was playing in the café. What I do understand, though, are the universal languages of sound. The sound that had nearly pulled my ears out of their sockets was a strange one. In words: 'dum, da da da dummm!' In sound, it is much more powerful and the Intel Pentium sonic logo, perhaps the most famous three seconds of music in the world, was the sound that took me 2,000 miles back to London and my job in commercial radio.

This was the moment at which I truly woke up to just how powerful sound can be as a communications tool for brands. I had always suspected it and some radio people had even been telling me for a while but there is nothing quite like an epiphany to punch-throw a metaphorical glass of water in your face, accompany it with a slap and bring you to your senses. Just over three seconds of technological-sounding music had grabbed my attention in a way no other marketing tool could have at that moment in Capri. I was in absolutely no mood to discuss computers, I was skint as a result of paying for the two coffees we were enjoying and I was not even listening. In fact, I was avoiding advertising and marketing completely because this was my honeymoon and I had spent the previous seven years saving up for it through my work in advertising and marketing.

As the Radio Advertising Bureau (RAB) would say, the ad I heard went in under the radar. That is to say, I did not know a company was communicating with me and I did not have a chance to put up the barriers. This, however, does not really explain the phenomenon. Far from going unnoticed on my communications radar, the Intel commercial showed up big, bright and bold. The other radio ads may have been communicating with me on some subconscious level (though with the language issue, I doubt it) but Intel's use of sound made me listen and made me pay attention. Radar or not, there was nothing I could do once I heard the sound except listen to the radio. The Intel sonic logo actually grabbed my attention and I had to consciously listen. This, I thought at the time and continue to do so, is an amazing thing. If all radio ads, I hypothesized, had sonic logos as different and recognizable as Intel's, then all radio ads would work so much more effectively. They would all force the listener to listen. That was just plain common sense as far as I was concerned so the real question that came to me was why is it only Intel and a few notable others that have a sonic logo?

I came home from my honeymoon and, after a little encouragement from those I counselled, set about setting up Sonicbrand with my business partner, Paul and latterly with Ali. Today, we still reference the way Intel uses sound, as a core part of its brand communications, when we are talking to our clients. It still has that same amazing effect of grabbing people when they are not listening and making them do so. It is a great example of the pure power of sound and is probably the most quoted sonic branding and the definitive sonic logo.

A logo is a symbol and Intel has a symbol in sound that is just as powerful as their symbol in graphics (more powerful according to our research). There are not many other companies or organizations that can say the same thing and yet almost every company today has access to sound-delivering channels for its communications. There are so few recognizable sonic logos in the world and yet there are thousands of recognizable graphic symbols knocking around. How do the organizations without sonic logos brand themselves in sound? Answer: inconsistently, inefficiently and ineffectively. The most basic level of argument I can make for why companies should invest a little time and money in sonic branding is that they are missing out on a slice of what Intel and some of the other biggest brands in the world have.

CHAPTER 1

The opportunity knocks

Sound is a very strong communicator. It does some very special things that no other communicator does. If a brand can identify opportunities for sonic communications and applies some of the art of sonic branding, it gains access to a whole world of communications opportunities that it never had before – like a café in Capri. Maybe your audiences are not in a café but on the beach or in their cars, listening to the radio, or in the kitchen, making a cup of tea but listening to the TV. Perhaps your audiences are on the telephone to your call centre or on your interactive voice recognition (IVR) portal. Perhaps your clients are in the cinema, watching and listening to ads or to the film and taking messages from them. There are other places your clients could be. They could be at their computer, visiting your website or they could be anywhere with a third generation mobile phone downloading content. They could be at a conference or an exhibition or watching a corporate video or opening sound-enabled product packaging. There are so many touchpoints today where we have the opportunity to communicate through sound that the imperative for putting some investment into how a company uses these channels has never been stronger.

As you can see in figure 1.1, there are at least 14 types of touchpoint where sound is a factor in the nature of experience. Of course, some are more important than others but which these are always depends upon the nature of the brand's relationship to its stakeholders. All the work that Sonicbrand has undertaken has involved the assessment and evaluation of every available touchpoint. Sometimes, the traditional channels are not open. For example, our work with Syngenta, a specialist agricultural manufacturer, initially involved the use of video and events only. The products we worked on did not advertise at the time, had no need for phone lines and had no retail environment.

What is quickly being realized is that it is impossible to brand sound-only environments with traditional logos or colours. With an increasing amount of business being conducted through call centres, an increasingly important touchpoint for many brands is the telephone. The Royal Institution of

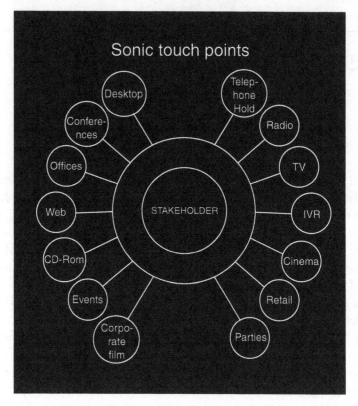

Figure 1.1   Sonic brand touchpoints

Chartered Surveyors (RICS), for example, conducts the vast majority of its work via the telephone, servicing its members and the public via its call centres. As a Sonicbrand client, RICS identified a need for it to express its brand and engage with its stakeholders. Given that there is an average on-hold time of more than five minutes while enquiries are being dealt with, the telephone hold system provided the best opportunity. The musical solution was successful and resonated with stakeholders to such an extent that many members requested copies for their own hold systems and the same music, in different guises, has become a theme for the brand across its other major touchpoints, including RICS events, conferences and awards ceremonies.

A traditional heartland for corporate communications is broadcast advertising. In its various guises from the 30-second spot to programming sponsorships, brands are given a short opportunity to engage with their audience. During our work with Powergen, the UK's leading energy supplier, most of the attention was given over to television advertising and the idents for their ITV channel weather sponsorships. The simple reason for this focus is that there are more stakeholder impacts generated by these channels, when they are used, than by any other. That said, the Powergen brand is far reaching and much thought had to be given to the telephone system and the sounds of desktop computers. Indeed, every touchpoint needed to be evaluated and brought into line with the sonic branding 'sound and feel'.

The Internet was heralded as providing great opportunities for pretty much everyone and that included the infant sonic branding industry. The full potential of the Internet as a brand communications touchpoint has probably yet to be realized and the lack of sound on the vast majority of websites is a part of its unfulfilled potential. The slow take-up of broadband services up to now has lead to the need for extremely small homepages and sonic branding has yet to really make its mark. In other words, we are still in the 'silent era' of the Web but 'talkies' are not far away.

Already, many sites have experimented with sound and taken advantage of today's music encoding software that allows small files with near-instant download on asymmetric digital subscriber lines (ADSL).

Sound-enabled websites are even common in some sectors, where a very high percentage of users have high-speed access. The UK media and marketing industry is very technologically advanced and, therefore, some of the brands that service this market have been able to make full use of sound on their websites. Perhaps the most apposite user of sonic branding is the Radio Advertising Bureau (RAB) in the United Kingdom. It has a sonic branding strategy that focuses on its website as its primary touchpoint with its stakeholders: media planners, buyers and marketeers. The RAB uses its sonic logo on a Flash title page for the website where its download size is easily accommodated.

Increasingly, we find that sonic branding projects are led by the retail environment. For all retailers, the store is the most important communications channel, far outweighing advertising in terms of the number of impacts and indeed the emotional impact of the experience. The latest understanding in this area is that the store should be seen and treated as a medium with a more sophisticated approach to content and programming. WPP, the brand and advertising group has set up its own internal department leading this thinking.

Music has long played a part in the retail environment but has largely failed to address issues of identity or consistency with other touchpoints. This is what sonic branding does for sound in a retail environment and it is a significant challenge. The kind of sonic logo employed by Direct Line is not currently welcome in-store where there is a desire to be far more subtle and gently persuasive. This is because staff and customers spend a long time in stores and there is a real danger of annoying them out of their minds if sonic branding is too obvious, too pervasive or just too irritating.

In the age of mobile communications, everywhere has become 'point of sale' and mobile phones and personal digital assistants (PDAs) are providing a range of opportunities for their users to interact and engage with brands. Indeed, future mobile devices will offer integrated phone, TV, radio and Web access and cause the media landscape in ten years from now to look very different indeed. One of the brands making early use of mobile communications as a brand touchpoint is Shazam Entertainment. It provides one of the breakthrough mobile phone technologies of today and gives users the ability to identify songs they hear on the radio, in a club or on TV, simply by dialling a short-code number on their phone and letting the computer on the other end take an audio fingerprint of the song. Shazam then sends a Short Message Service (SMS) to the mobile phone with the name of the song and artist, at the same time putting a link on your personal Shazam web-page that facilitates purchase of the song through Amazon.

This is interesting for a number of reasons. First, it demonstrates how music is driving the use of mobile technologies; second, it is in an indication of how music and technology have become inextricably linked; and third it presented Sonicbrand with the intriguing challenge of creating a brand experience through the primary touchpoint of a mobile phone. The brief to identify the brand and convey its attitude in just a few seconds was relatively simple but the challenge of creating an IVR portal that was engaging and on-brand was far greater. The answer lay in the use of smart sound design, music and voice.

A very different brief given to Sonicbrand in 2000 was to help create free-thinking zones for Reuter's executives using sound. In fact, corporate meeting rooms are a touchpoint of increasing importance as many companies seek to move away from the austere boardroom to a more organic, person-friendly environment. By mixing some classically relaxing ambient sounds such as wind and rain with a variety of emotive music, we were able to give analytically minded, stressed-out corporate types a little taste of mental freedom within their working day and fresh ideas were allowed to flow freely.

Though we categorize touchpoints, in reality, each time we work with a new client we find a completely new set of challenges and an enormous realm of opportunity for brands to convey their emotional messages and build belief and trust among stakeholders. The theme that runs through every sonic branding project, however, is that no matter what the fundamental touchpoint, all touchpoints should be brought into line to generate a consistent sound and feel. Only by achieving this communications multiple is a brand really able to make the most of its sonic opportunities.

The number of sonic touchpoints available and the complexity of the stakeholder's journey through his or her day, mean that the world of sonic branding has never been more diverse and potentially confusing. As a result, this new discipline is currently being interpreted, creatively, in many different ways by many different companies. A large proportion of the businesses and individuals who have jumped upon the bandwagon are composers who assert that if they write music for a brand, it must be sonic branding. Though they are undoubtedly working within the industry, the creation of music is not in itself sonic branding.

It is vital to remember that the essence of sonic branding is twofold: the creation of brand expressions in sound and the consistent, strategic usage of these properties across touchpoints. Sonic branding choices must be informed as much by the strategic approach as by the creative execution and the salient points when assessing the offerings of sonic branding suppliers should be strategic and creative. It really does not matter whether the brand expression proposed is a symphony or a jingle as both may sometimes be appropriate, the primary opportunity is in the strategic management of the right creative property, no matter what it is. This is the approach that sets sonic branding apart from those who have gone before and use the terms with little understanding for their meaning.

In the past, creative choices have generally dominated over strategy in the choice of music and sound, particularly in the realms of television and radio. These are the media where most sound has been used by brands, in some of its least subtle and most affecting forms but they are also the media that have created the opportunity for a much sung but currently unloved form of sonic branding; the jingle.

A jingle is a short slogan, verse or tune designed to be easily remembered. As defined above, a jingle is not in itself sonic branding but if it is consistently managed it can become an incredibly powerful component of sonic branding. A jingle is one of the devices available for asking stakeholders to behave or act in a desired way. It usually has a single purpose – to be memorable – and is a sign for the brand whereas the logo is a symbol. The jingle is a mnemonic (intended to help the memory); the sonic logo a vessel for associations. The word and the concept of jingles seem to be out of vogue with the advertising industry that used them so effectively for so long. Why this has happened is open to debate but 'jingle fatigue'[1] has been cited as a factor among ad people. Also, it has been proposed that jingles are too obviously a sales message and thereby too easily filtered out by today's discerning consumer.

While the former argument probably had some merit in the 1970s, in no way could the market be said to be saturated with jingles today. Similarly, the latter point, though interesting, seems unlikely. The essence of the jingle is that it is almost impossible to filter because of the way rhyme and melody are employed to creep into the audience's head. In fact, the Germans have their own word for jingle, *ohrworm*, literally 'ear-worm'. A more likely explanation of why jingles are not employed by the UK ad industry is a general lack of understanding of how music works as a communications tool. There is a dearth of musically trained creatives and a subsequent lack of sophistication in the choice of music for ads. Music is generally left to last, subjugated beneath the visual interpretation of TV commercials. As a result, musical choices are made quickly and there has been a well-documented history of track choices coming down to what happens to be playing on the creative director's CD at the time. The phenomenon of acts such as Moby, who licensed most of the tracks on his album, Play and Röyksopp, who are currently in vogue with the ad world is born from the fashion approach to music by ad agencies.

In the US, it seems that good ideas are not easily abandoned by ad creatives. The American ad industry has not so slavishly followed the 'ads as art' path of the UK and still favours effective communications rather than thought-provoking cryptic commercials. As a result, the jingle has never lost its place in the US industry or in the minds of the American public. Their time may even be coming again in the UK. One of the most important campaigns of 2002 was for the home furnishings store, Ikea. Created by Karmarama, a small, new, London-based agency, the ads featured the jingle 'It's time to live unlimited'. It will be interesting to see whether the agency and client realize how important that mnemonic has become and seek to retain it in the face of pressure to be constantly new.

At Sonicbrand, we have a lot of time for jingles and they have an important place in the history and future of the discipline. So, we will examine the nature of jingles and their place in the history of brands and culture. Apart from their rich heritage, there really is no room for a snobbish attitude to jingles for one overarching reason; they work. Together with other commissioned and licenced music, they are frontline tools in advertising and always have been.

CHAPTER 2

Jingle all the way

The history of marketing and advertising is full of fascinating examples of how companies have employed music as a part of their communications activities. Though in many areas they were copying existing art-forms such as the movies or commercial radio, in some instances the ad industry actually lead the cultural development of the western world.

The first documentary evidence I can find of a business using a sound-only medium for marketing purposes comes from an article in the *Western Electrician*, dated 12 September 1903. It reported that a store in Fairmont, Minnesota, had more success soliciting for business using the telephone than by 'sending clerks or errand boys'.[1] So, telephone canvassing is 100 years old. We must organize a party. The earliest example of a piece of music being used for the advertising and promotion of a company, as far as the very sketchy history goes, is from 1905 in the United States. As the automobile culture grew, a man named Gus Edwards wrote the music for a song whose lyrics are attributed to Vincent P. Bryan. The song became famous among enthusiastic fans of the cars made by Oldsmobile. It was called 'In my merry Oldsmobile' and in 1908, recognizing its strength as an anthem, the Oldsmobile Motor Company adopted the song for use in its marketing communications.

Predating this, however, was the cultural phenomenon of the jingle and it was here that the ad world took the lead. From around 1900 onwards, the jingle was seen as being the very height of cultural sophistication. In those days, jingles always had rhymed verses, designed to aid the memorability of brands like Force cereal. They also became popular entertainment with jingle-writing becoming a national pastime in the US.

The Force cereal jingle

Jim Dumps was a most unpleasant man
Who lived his life on a hermit's plan
He'd never stop for a friendly smile
But trudged along in his moody style

Till 'Force' one day was served to him
Since then they call him 'Sunny Jim'.

The development of the jingle stalled for a while, until it found its new and truest home; commercial radio.

From the early 1920s onwards, commercial radio in the United States became the obvious vehicle for companies who wanted to use music to promote their services. During the medium's early development, it was prevented from being used as a direct advertising medium, however, due in many respects to the newspapers and magazines of the time. Fearing the competition that commercial radio would pose if it were allowed to attract advertising dollars, the press ran campaigns to keep the airways ad free. As a result, until the Depression but also well beyond it, commercial messages in the radio were carried by sponsored bands and orchestras such as the Royal Typewriter Salon Orchestra, the Cliquot Club Eskimos and the Vick's Vap-o-rub Quartet. These groups played music suitable for the times and suitable for their benefactors. Palmolive Soap even went as far as to rename the solo artistes that they sponsored. Thus Frank Munn became Paul Oliver and Virginia Rae became Olive Palmer. This was to create ownership and differentiation. Existing stars with existing names had existing associations and connotations. These 'newly created' singers belonged only to Palmolive.

As an interesting historical aside, it was during the 1920s that 'crooning' was invented. It was a style of singing that stayed within the mid-ranges of the voice, avoiding the highest tenor and soprano notes that the transmitter tubes and crystal set radio receivers could not handle.

So, the 1920s saw the growth of companies using music to communicate with customers but it also saw a boom in the use of music as an internal communications tool. In much the same way as the colliery brass bands had created strong bonds between business and its working communities, American industry in the 1920s sought to harness the power of music, to bind it to and motivate its workers. Department stores were particularly active in this respect, perhaps as a result of the theatrical nature of their offering. Macy's, for example, would have a group singsong before they opened the doors for a sale. They also put on an annual company musical performed by staff, for staff.

In the 1930s, corporate America was looking to expand the sales of its goods to more rural areas and music radio proved the perfect vehicle. Country music was identified by many companies as being a credible way to sell new products to an old-fashioned, rural audience. Alka-Seltzer and Black Draught (a beautifully named laxative) were two of the major sponsors of country music radio stations at the time.

Also in the 1930s, General George Squire patented a method of delivering music down telegraph wires. General George's invention was extremely hi-tech for the times and when he came to name the company under which he would market his product, he took inspiration from his favourite existing technology brand – Kodak, and the essence of his offering – music. The composite of the two words gave him and the world the phenomenon of Muzak, which has since become a generic for a certain genre of easy-listening music, often heard in hotel lobbies. According to the official history of the company, which today boasts the largest listenership of any music medium in the world, Muzak was widely employed in American industry throughout the 1940s to manipulate the feelings of factory and office workers. It soothed the minds and was said to enhance production.

Muzak's 'killer application' however, was handed to it by the architects and builders of the great steel skyscrapers of the 1920s and 1930s. Buildings had never been built that high before and people at the time were naturally scared of getting in new-fangled elevators that took them up to 100 storeys above the city. Muzak was fed into the elevators as it had a calming effect, taking passengers' minds off the fact that they were dangling perilously above the city. The soothing sounds became famous, known the world over as 'elevator music'.

Through the 1940 and 1950s, Muzak became more complex and scientific. Taking a research-based approach, Muzak identified that music in the workplace improved morale, productivity and even workforce attendance records. They also introduced the idea of 'stimulus progression' where the intensity of music would be changed according to the time of day. McDonald's and more recently by AsSeenOnScreen, one of the UK's leading Web retailers, would later adopt this approach.

Throughout the 1940s, the jingle culture continued to develop. 'Pepsi-Cola Hits the Spot' (words and adaptation by Austen Herbert Croom-Johnson and Alan Bradley Kent) was the first network radio jingle. It was made into a record and over one million copies of the jingle were successfully placed in jukeboxes around the United States. Even more popular, perhaps, than Pepsi, was the jingle for Chiquita Bananas, a brand of the United Fruit Company. It was created by the advertising agency BBDO by Ken Mackenzie and Garth Montgomery under the guidance of Robert Foreman. At the height of its musical popularity, it was played 376 times in one day on one radio station. It was so famous that it was recorded three times by different artists and sold almost one million copies, as well as being a juke-box hit like Pepsi.

In the 1950s, the United Kingdom joined the party. The first jingles were heard on the new ITV channel and became famous overnight. Ask anyone of a certain age if they 'wonder where the yellow went?' The reply of Pepsodent will be instant. Similarly, in those days, apparently, just 'a little dab would do ya' when it came to applying Brylcream. Pepsodent and Brylcream were both brands and jingles from the United States.

The 1960s, 1970s and 1980s saw a demise in the creation and use of jingles and a switch towards limited licensing of whole songs by existing artists, the rationale being that the inclusion of a song on an ad usually created a large volume of sales for the record company. The other undoubted benefit of this strategy was the perceived endorsement of a product by the artist behind the music. This dovetailed well with the overall move towards endorsement advertising of the era.

Some very famous artists' records have been used to the great profit of the artists and record companies if not, necessarily, to the brands. Coca-Cola, a brand with a rich heritage of music licensing, has taken tracks from the likes of the Everly Brothers, the Supremes and even Marvin Gaye. It says much for how their understanding of sonic branding has developed, however, that since the early 1970s, Coke has used original music. In fact, in 1971, Coke had probably the greatest hit in sonic branding history. The music for their ad campaign, entitled 'I'd like to buy the world a Coke' was reworded and released by the New Seekers as 'I'd Like to Teach the World to Sing (in perfect harmony)'. It was a global smash that is forever associated with the brand. As a child of the 1970s, I even remember being taught this song in my school choir. Is it a wonder that I still drink the stuff today?

Though Coke learned the potential profits of commissioning their own music as much as 30 years ago, most other brands are yet to learn and spend vast sums on famous music for their ads. A selection of the most famous would include 'Start Me Up' by the Rolling Stones in Microsoft ads, 'Blue Suede Shoes' sung by Elvis in Apple's Mac ads and 'Revolution' by The Beatles as used by Nike. This practice continues today and dominates the approach that advertising agencies take towards the use of music for their clients. The limited licence (limited by time, territory and medium), of course, still suits the record companies and the advertising agencies. If clients need to renew or purchase a new licence every year, then the record companies and ad agencies have a guaranteed earner.

Sonicbrand believes that the practice of limited licensing of existing music for advertising is an outmoded method of conduct that is clung onto by ad agencies and record companies partly for the revenues it generates and partly through lack of knowledge and inertia. While the benefits for these two industries are clear – and tactically it can be of value to hit chart success with the soundtrack to an ad – they would appear to be short term. As soon as the campaign that made a song famous is off-air, the song lives on, with its identity and associations reverting to the artist. Levi's, one of the most famous music licensors of the 1980s, created many hits for many artists but after the parade was left with no enduring brand properties. The same can be said for countless other brands. Licensing is short term and the real question is, what are the long-term benefits for the brand? There is little value for money, there is little chance for consistency between media, region and audiences or over time and a licensed track makes the music the star, not the brand.

The jingle ethos of the 1920s, whereby companies commissioned and owned their own music, is an ethos that the sonic branding industry is starting to revive. If a brand-owner has the foresight to commission their own sonic branding, then they have the right to expect that they will not be held to ransom by limited licences.

CHAPTER 3

What the movies did for us

John Williams became the shark I did not have available to me in that movie.

Steven Spielberg on *Jaws*[1]

We have seen that jingles and music have long been employed by the advertising and marketing communities to help get their messages across but there is much, much more to sonic branding than the 30-second TV or radio spot. Indeed, the most important area of our culture, in relation to how music and sound influence how we feel, is far removed from the world of advertising.

Artistically, the area that we reference the most in our creative processes and product is the film industry. The role of sound in films is to enhance the experience, make the action more believable and make it more memorable. This, coincidentally, is also a major role of music in branding. The development of talking pictures, which coincided with the development of music and brands gives a fascinating insight into how technology and composition techniques were developed to convey every kind of emotion through sound. Films have become a common cultural experience and have created a language of musical archetypes that we can harness for enhancing elements of the brand experience. Just think again of the stabbing scene in *Psycho* or music from *Jaws*. These and many others are clichés that we can use to create emotional reactions in almost any audience and the movies gave them to us. Film was undeniably one of the most influential media of the twentieth century and its influence continues to grow. The full history of film is interesting but there is one particular aspect that is directly linked with sonic branding and that is the way that the cinema has employed sound, music especially, to enhance the medium and create the most engaging art-form we have.

It did not take a man of genius to realize that silent movies were all very well but pictures with sound could be much more powerful. Nonetheless, it was a genius, Thomas Edison, who started trying to synchronize moving pictures and sound in the 1880s. His experiments with the kinetograph and kinetophone were successful in that he managed to accurately synchronize recorded sound with pictures. Edison is, thus, credited with the invention of pretty much everything to do with recorded sound. Where Edison was not successful was in the quality of the sound. In fact, the quality of the sound from his wax-cylinder recordings was so low as to be almost impossible to listen to for any considerable length of time. Edison's other failing was that he was working with very short films and recordings but we can forgive him for this because he was, after all, pioneering an art-form that dominates cultures all over the world today.

The world's first public cinema was opened in Paris in 1896 and it heralded a great period in motion pictures; the silent era. This is something of a misnomer, though, because the experience for the early cinema audiences was anything but silent. Early accounts from early film-goers speak of the disjointed and disconcerting experience of seeing people talking and horses galloping and yet hearing nothing at all. Audiences were apt to talk and lose their concentration so the Lumière brothers, pioneers of cinema in France in the late nineteenth century, recognized very quickly that they needed to add some sound to their cinematic presentations in order to keep their audiences riveted.

Where Edison's experiments with synchronous pre-recorded sound were not very satisfying, the Lumières had the notion to use live sound in the cinema and this was far more successful. In 1896, in both Paris and London, the Lumières employed an orchestra to play along with their short films. The success of these shows lead to it becoming widely understood by cinema owners all over Europe and the United States that some kind of musical accompaniment was beneficial during picture shows. It is easy to imagine how effective the combination of a live orchestra and moving pictures must have been in the early years of the last century. In fact, the combination is still a powerful one, as demonstrated, for example, in 2002 by the BBC's *Blue Planet* open-air concert. To this end, cinemas adopted music and sound techniques from the theatre and employed house musicians and singers. Largely, they played standard popular music of the age, be it Bach or music hall. Music added another dimension to the experience, even if it was not related dramatically to the visuals. Its mere presence was enough to help suspend the disbelief of the audience, allowing them to become more involved with the pictures on the screen.

Music 'fake books' were an early attempt to establish a consistent approach to conveying distinct emotions through music. Volumes such as the *Kinobibliotech* by Guiseppe Becce and *The Sam Fox Moving Picture Music Volumes* by J. S. Zamecnik, were made up of sheet music organized by emotion. Thus, pieces of music were written with titles such as 'Night: sinister mood' and 'Night: threatening mood'. According to the judgement of the cinema musicians, these could be played to support the scenes on screen. Though largely viewed as clichéd today, at the time the ideas within these volumes became the foundations for matching music with movie scenes. The obvious limitations of these books, though, lay in the fact that the same piece of music would be played over any film that had similar scenes.

The first bespoke film score is believed to have been written by Camille Saint-Saëns in 1908 for the French film *L'assassinat du Duc de Guise*. This was a major step into the future of film music as it was written to reflect and enhance the emotional context of a specific film. Saint-Saëns, however, was expensive and the idea of commissioning original music was shelved for some years. Of course, orchestras were also expensive and many smaller cinemas could not afford them. Often, however, they could afford to buy an organ, which became the instrument of choice because of its greatly amplified sounds and the ability of the organist to create great shades of light and dark in the sound that the instrument makes.

While live music was supporting and enhancing the growing film business and must have been extremely effective as an art-form, it was a very expensive and exclusive art, available only to the rich in the biggest metropolitan centres. In the US, musicianship centred upon New York, which meant that only in New York could a mass audience experience films the way they were meant to seen and heard. Outside of the big cities, smaller audiences meant that large orchestras could not be afforded. Though some had organs, cinemas without music proved unpopular. It was obvious to film-makers that the full orchestral score added significantly to the art-form and without it film just was not that interesting. The imperative was to find a cheap way to synchronize recorded music and pictures so that nation-wide audiences could feel the full effect of the orchestra.

Experiments aimed at using pre-recorded sound with the movies had been started and abandoned by Edison, but many people continued where he left off. Some weird and wonderful mechanical techniques were tried, including linking projectors and phonograph records with long pulleys and asking projectionists to manually turn the film at speeds specified by measures on special phonographs. While these varying methods worked satisfactorily, they did not synchronize accurately and were thus limited. As a result, no one method became standard or available on a broad commercial scale until the mid-1920s.

By 1925, a consortium led by Warner Bros had developed new technology called the Vitaphone. It was the first system to allow good quality music to be played back perfectly synchronized with pictures. On 6 August of that year, in the 'refrigerated' Warner Theatre on Broadway, New York City, *Don Juan*, featuring major stars John Barrymore and Mary Astor was released. It was an experimental film that used the Vitaphone technique in a limited way. It was shot in the same way as any other silent movie of the era in that there was no dialogue, but the addition of a pre-recorded orchestral score made the film the first of the age of sound. The film showcased the talent of the New York Philharmonic, one of the finest orchestras of the day.

The musical film was well received and Warners set about their next release which was again to be a film shot in the silent style, with no dialogue and plot lines showed on narration cards. The movie they made starred one of the biggest stars of popular entertainment in the United States at that time, Al Jolson. It was called *The Jazz Singer* and it was conceived, like *Don Juan*, to showcase music. Film-makers were at the time very sceptical as to whether characters on film should talk. The scepticism came from a Luddite 'if it ain't broke don't fix it' attitude to the film business and also from the sheer volume of logistical problems that would have to be overcome in order to make talking pictures. Silent movies could be shot anywhere but talking pictures would require silent stages, actors tied with wires to recorders and a big chunk of investment. A great representation of these times is contained in the film *Singing in the Rain*.

Apart from his offensive make-up and sentimentality, Al Jolson's great contribution to cinema was the result of the ad-lib comments he made during the shooting and recording of *The Jazz Singer*. Before and after the songs, he said a few words, some of which were witty. Warners left these ad-libs in the movie and when it hit cinemas the effect was amazing. The ad-libs became incredibly popular. Audiences loved seeing Jolson talk and showed it through their ticket purchases. The film took over $100,000 per week in 1927, an unprecedented amount. Money like that convinced the sceptics very quickly and all of a sudden, most of the major studios switched their production away from silent films to 'talkies'. Warners, of course, were ahead of the game and they had another huge talkie hit in 1928 with *The Singing Fool*. Tickets cost $11 and on a production budget of $200,000 it took over $5 million in sales. Talkies became big business and heralded the birth of the modern era of cinema. They also continued to raise the stakes at the box office, in other words, they made the cinema much more popular. In 1927, with only *The Jazz Singer* representing talkies, the total US box office was $57 million. By 1930, this had increased to $110 million.

It was a good job, there was so much money flying in, because making talkies proved extremely difficult and expensive. The technology of the time only allowed one recording to be made. The music, therefore, had to be recorded live, with the actors. This meant the presence of orchestras on-stage. Of course, if one violinist made a mistake, the whole scene would have to be re-shot. There are accounts of three day shoots for one song. The expense was accompanied by a lack of experience and knowledge of how the audience would react to the music. For some years it was believed that the music had to be represented visually in some way for the audience to believe in it. This led to the incongruous appearance of gypsy violinists and randomly placed bands of musicians who seemed to appear at exactly the moment that music was required and then disappear. Pretty much all of the first talkies were musicals. Primarily, these gave an excuse for the orchestra to be on stage; they were also jumping upon *The Jazz Singer* bandwagon. As with all popular things, however, the bubble burst and it did so at the time of the Great Depression in the United States.

The 1930s was a period of great experimentation for music in cinema as audiences demanded more spoken words and less prancing and dancing. Composers were asked, like Sans-Saëns, to write original scores that would support the drama of the piece. This was important, because the technical requirements of making talkies required very conservative use of cameras and studio-bound actors. Thus, music had to make up for the rather boring visuals of early talkies. Musicians were also given freedom, for the first time, to work away from the rest of the shoot. The technology to re-record and dub music and spoken words together in an editing suite arrived, which meant that films could be shot without the restrictions of having the orchestra in the studio or on film. This made a big difference to the production process, allowing more complex music to be added to the film while lowering the costs. Music became standard in the cinema as a result and the 1930s saw the first guidelines laid down for how cinemas should present films aurally. The Academy Curve was developed and defined for the positioning of speakers in studios and cinemas, allowing film-makers to create and listen to the sound in the same way as their audience.

The 1940s was a golden era for movies and music. One of the most famous films of the period was Disney's *Fantasia*. It was a musical and animation tour de force starring Mickey Mouse. Apart from its cultural impact, mixing the best animation with fantastic music, it was also the first film ever created with multichannel surround sound, recorded with live multitracking. The drive towards surround sound came from the film-maker's desire to have sound events follow the characters around the screen, which added a new level of realism to the cinema experience.

Fantasound was developed from scratch as a whole new technology. As well as the new recording processes and equipment required, a new set-up was needed in the cinemas in order for it to work. To kit out a cinema with

Fantasound cost over $85,000 and involved the placing of 54 speakers. Unsurprisingly, only two systems were ever installed, though a roadshow version was developed which wowed audiences all over the US. Despite its lack of commercial success, the principles of Fantasound, with different channels relating to different parts of the screen and space, was the inspiration for all the surround sound systems that amaze us today.

Citizen Kane, in 1941, broke the mould in storytelling, camerawork and sound. Bernard Herrmann wrote the score and is said to have been ten years ahead of anyone else in the movie industry, employing textures and contemporary sounds before most composers or listeners considered them to be applicable to music.

Another interesting 1940s film was *The Lost Weekend* starring Ray Milland and Jane Wyman, directed by the great Billy Wilder. This was a trailblazing movie depicting alcoholism and was originally released with no music at all. This was deliberate, creatively, as the film's script and camerawork were outstanding and the absence of music, it was felt, would create a necessary darkness of atmosphere. The first audiences, however, did not react quite as anticipated. In the darkest scenes, where Milland is falling into an alcoholic blur, the audience actually laughed and giggled. It is thought that they behaved this way because they felt uncomfortable and simply did not know how to react. The producers, however, thought that the situation was serious enough to stop the film being released.[2] Miklos Rosza was called in to save and score the film so the release could take place. With the new soundtrack, audiences felt the emotional pain that Milland felt and they knew how to react. The film went on to be one of the biggest hits of the year and won six Academy Awards including Best Score for Rosza, who would go on to create the outstanding scores for classic movies such as *El Cid*, *Quo Vadis* and *Ben Hur*.

The 1950s saw little new technology in film sound and creatively film scoring had a hard time catching up with the innovations of the 1940s. Cinema also came under massive threat from television, which started to dominate popular culture. The best cinema owners could do was to introduce various widescreen formats but they did little to stem the flow of audiences away from theatres and into their armchairs. Studios sacked their in-house orchestras and composers (just as cinemas had done with the birth of talkies) and looked for new ways to innovate and win back audiences. In 1951, *A Streetcar Named Desire* was heralded for its score, because it brought jazz, the popular music of the age, to the screen. 1953's *East of Eden* did the same and just a few years later the move to popular music was complete when the cinema discovered rock'n'roll. In 1956, Elvis starred in *Love Me Tender*, singing the hit theme song and bringing millions of teenagers to the cinema. His career in Hollywood was apocryphal, starting as a credible artist and ending as an exploited puppet, but he showed more than any other performer how powerful the combination of moving pictures and music could be. In most ways, his film forays were the forerunners to the music video but as well as heralding a new art-form his debut marked the end of the golden era of movie music, the heights of which are rarely achieved today.

Much of the development since the 1950s has been technological. In 1971, Stanley Kubrick's *A Clockwork Orange* was the first movie to use Dolby A noise reduction, which took the 'hiss' out of the sound. This became a standard process for film soundtracks. Kubrick was a great fan of music and sound, believing them to be one of the best ways to convey and reinforce messages to an audience. Just watch and listen to the opening of *2001, A Space Odyssey* to understand why.

Science fiction movies have generally pushed the boundaries for movie sound as each effects team has sought to outdo the other. *Star Wars* (1977), *Battlestar Galactica* (1978), *Return of the Jedi* (1983) and *Robocop* (1986) were all landmark films for surround sound and serious bass.

Since film scoring became common practice in the 1940s, films have been created to convey every human emotion and all of them have employed music and sound to convey that emotion. Our culture has, there-fore, a vast back catalogue of music that matches almost every circumstance and emotion imaginable. Unsurprisingly, this body of work is a great place to look for inspiration when examining the kind of music that a brand could use to express itself. As a result, soundtracks are a staple of the moodboards at the heart of the creative process for sonic branding.

CHAPTER 4

What is sonic?

The development of the marketing and movie industries over the last 100 years informs much of what we call sonic branding. The obvious connection is the way in which these two industries have used the power of sound in its various guises and in the following chapter we will start to unravel the medium of sound itself. The goal is to understand its mechanics and its relationship with humanity, so that we can fully harness the power of sound. Just before we get into things, it is worth stating that for our purposes the words 'sound' and 'sonic' mean the same things. Sonic branding has been chosen by the industry as the generic for little reason other than it just sounds sexier than 'sound'. Why this is so is a matter for phonetics and linguistics and possibly another book.

At Sonicbrand, we like to demystify things and that means we are big on definitions. The broadest technical definition of 'sonic' is that it relates to any wave or vibration that has a frequency within the audible range of the human ear. In layman's terms, sonic is anything you can hear. This simple definition understates things a little but as you can probably already tell, I think sound is actually very exciting. It is also complex and something that we should really be grateful to receive. Sound is our warning sense – we can shut our eyes but we cannot shut our ears. It is also a compassionate sense because sound gives us the opportunity to listen. Sound is your baby crying (and someone else's) and sound is hearing your partner say 'I do'. Sound is birdsong and whale song and police sirens. It is the wind in the trees and baby gerbils 'clicking'. It is what makes the cinema a great experience and what makes car alarms a pain in the neck.

Sound, created by people, is what makes the atmosphere in a football stadium. I had the misfortune to be invited to an executive box at Stamford Bridge, the home of Chelsea Football Club, a few years ago. At the end of our stodgy meal, my colleagues and I were ushered into the glass-enclosed viewing area. It was double-glazed and silent. Outside, 30,000 fans were screaming but all I could hear was the shuffling of those around me. The game kicked off and those in the box suspected that the meal had been laced with tranquillizers. I can safely say that being isolated from the sound of the crowd took away 99% of the excitement of watching the game. After a few minutes the smart stewards remembered to turn on the speakers and we were treated to an audio feed from the ground. Suddenly, I and my fellow VIPs were actually at a football match and were able to enjoy watching Arsenal FC win handsomely.

Sound provides the atmosphere in many media as well. I tried an experiment at home with a video-recorded copy of Michael Owen's wondergoal for England versus Argentina at the World Cup 1998. With the sound on, the video clip still makes my hair stand on end. When I hit the mute button all the drama seems to drain away. The same things still happen; a cute first touch, a drop of the shoulder and a reverse shot, but the emotion is gone. It turns out that sound conveys the emotion while the pictures convey the information.

If sound's role in football is not enough to convince you that it is exciting stuff, then how about this? Sound is music and music is magic. For me music does not get any better than Elvis Presley singing 'Suspicious Minds' or hearing Debussy's 'Clare De Lune' played live; but while musical taste is personal, delight in music is universal.

In order to understand more about the relationship between people and music, I conducted a survey of some 130 of my closest friends. I asked this broad cross-section of the middle classes some questions about their CD or vinyl collections. The first question was 'Do you have a CD or record collection?' Amazingly, every person I asked, under the age of sixty, has said yes. That, in itself, is staggering. Does everyone you know have a stamp collection or a model car collection? I suspect the answer is 'no' but maybe stamps or model cars are not fair comparisons. To compare like with like, does anyone you know have an art or sculpture collection to match their record collection? Music collections just seem to be a part of everybody's life, they are a universal hobby and a fantastic source of social interaction, conversations and birthday presents.

The next question was 'Why do you have a music collection?' Apart from the basic, 'I like music' answers, many people were extremely eloquent and detailed in their responses. One of the most interesting reasons given for why people own music collections is that the selection of music defines the person. Each CD in a collection represents a year or a friend or a lover. It is as if the rack next to the stereo is proof of a life lived. In this sense, music collections seem to have taken the place of the scrapbook or even photo album as a way of recalling the good times. It is particularly interesting to me that so many of the people I asked were keen to regale me of their entire collection. Often I was given details of the way the music was classified (a generally male response) and the more expressive went so far as to tell me about their favourite tracks and how they reminded them of being 11 years old and standing at a school disco.

Roger Hyslop – the esteemed chairman of Triangle Group, the advertising and retail communications specialist – sent me what amounted to a musically annotated story of his life. It seems that he is unable to talk about his record collection without being drawn into discussing the personal experiences and rights of passage that accompanied every Fats Domino, Elvis and Beatles record. I am the same. From the moment I heard Elvis singing 'King Creole' ('Dixieland Rock' on the B-side) from my mother's record collection, I was hooked and some of my earliest memories are accompanied in my head by the sound of Elvis at Madison Square Garden, 1972, playing on my parent's old Sony music-centre. Today, my record collection has more Elvis than you can shake a stick at, because our first musical influences, the ones we encounter early in life, come to dominate our collections. All my respondents' collections majored on the music from their youth with very few having more new stuff than old. The 30-somethings told me that they had been filling in the gaps in their collections more than adding new music since they hit their late 20s. Interestingly, most of the teenagers I spoke to had very varied collections that ranged from Sinatra to the most modern pop acts. If the pop reality TV phenomenon is doing anything that is beneficial for music it must be that it is introducing new generations to the great songs of the 1950s and 1960s.

The last question I asked provided some staggering statistics. I asked how many CDs or records people owned? Answers ranged around 20 for the youngest respondents and averaged around 150 for everyone else. Darren Tate, a composer and DJ, owns more than 2,000 individual CD albums and too many vinyl records to count. He is in the enviable position of being given free music because of his place in the industry. As a result, however, he has little emotional attachment to most of his collection. The biggest 'private' collection amongst my respondents was 6,000 CDs and records. I find these numbers astounding but they also make sense to me.

Anyone who grew up in the late 1950s witnessed the birth of rock'n'roll and it clearly made an enormous impact upon many of them. For them, record buying was secondary to hearing it live at Saturday night dances. As souvenirs of great nights out, record sales boomed and by the time that generation matured, their desire to buy music was firmly established and grew throughout the 1960s. The early 1970s saw the birth of commercial music radio in the UK. Capital Radio London and Radio Clyde Glasgow kicked us off and my generation was born into a world of wall-to-wall music, radios in our bedrooms and hand-me-down record players. Anyone in their

30s has grown up surrounded by music. We were the first generation to have mobile music through the revolutionary Sony Walkman. We took our music with us everywhere and listened alone. Commercial radio was joined by MTV. Vinyl and compact cassette were joined by CD and more recently the MP3 phenomenon. This saw thousands of people reaching for Napster in an attempt to 'try before you buy' or find the rare tunes from their youth that had long been deleted from record label distribution.

In a smaller way, even the generation before rock'n'roll was besotted with music. Though my granny, at 86 years old, has no music collection besides a couple of music boxes, when she was growing up, she had a classic 'trumpet' record player. Recorded music was for the wealthy enthusiast in the 1920s but many households could afford a few records and would gather round to listen. Hi-fi was still a long way off but just to hear the scratchy reproduction was a special treat. Most people, however, only heard music on the wireless, which sounded more like a tin can on a string than today's crystal clear Digital Audio Broadcast (DAB) systems.

How much richer are our lives because of the proliferation of high-quality music on request, 24 hours a day? We really do have to appreciate the technological advances of the last 50 years that have made this possible. Imagine going back to a world where the only music you heard was through a single speaker longwave radio? And talking of longwave, we all love sound so much these days that the number of radios per household in the UK averages around six.[1] Radios are devices whose only function is to let us hear interesting sounds.

CHAPTER 5

The sciency bit

Sound has a number of qualities, most of them extremely useful and all of them interesting in their own way. One of the most remarkable aspects of sound is that it is a science. Understanding its nature requires some very brief lessons in physics and biology.

What humans hear is any sound within the audible frequency, roughly between 20 Hz and 20 kHz. Herz is the Standard International (SI) unit of frequency, equal to one cycle per second. It is named for Heinrich Rudolph Herz, a German physicist and one of the pioneers of radio transmission. These sounds are carried by alternating waves of compression and rarefaction in an elastic medium for example, air or water, after having been generated by a sound source. Sound, of course, has a speed and it is quite fast, though not as fast as light. I remember the first time I learned about the speed of sound. I was eight years old and a forgotten school teacher took a bunch of kids into the playground. A couple of hundred metres away, one kid held a gong above his head and the rest of us saw him strike it. A moment later, we heard the sound. This was one of my first science lessons and it made quite an impression. The wait for the sound was less than half a second but more than enough to fascinate a bunch of eight-year-olds. The vision of our classmate striking the gong reached us at about 299 million metres per second. Very fast indeed. The much more relaxed sound component reached us at a far more leisurely speed of 345 metres per second.

The amount of sound, or the volume to you and me, is actually a physical quantity made up of the differing elements of sound power, sound intensity and sound pressure. It is usually expressed in decibels, which have no dimension themselves but are relative to a specified reference value. Sound power, like other measures of power, is a function of energy and time. In this case, it is a measurement of how much acoustic energy (expressed in joules) is transferred to the surrounding medium per second. Sound intensity, usually expressed in terms of watts per square metre, is a measure of how much acoustic energy is present in any physical area, any distance from the sound source.

Finally, sound pressure refers to the change in pressure within the medium when sound is present. This is usually expressed as pascals (abbreviated Pa) which are equal to one newton per square metre. Pressure is always a function of the amount of weight pressing on an area. For example, a relatively small press on a pin will create a lot of pressure on a very small area of a cork-board and allow the pin to penetrate the cork's surface. The same weight of press with your thumb, without the pin, will not penetrate the cork as the pressure is spread over a larger area and is thus dissipated.

So, sound comes from a source, travels through a medium at 345 metres per second and then hits our ears. This is where we get into a little biology. The first bit of kit that we possess for hearing sounds is the pinna or outer ear. Pinna is a word derived from the Latin for feather, wing or fin and though some people's ears can tend to look more like wings than anything else, they actually do a good job of capturing sounds and directing them towards the business end, which starts with the auditory canal. This is the bit of the ear you can reach with a cotton bud, though medical science would tell you not to. Here, sound is amplified by a factor of two.

From there, the sound is directed via the tympanis membrane, usually called the eardrum, and into the ossicles, which helps softer sounds to be amplified.

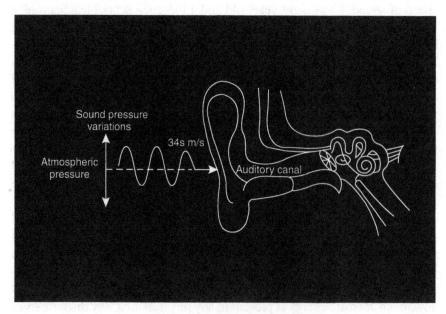

Figure 5.1 The outer ear

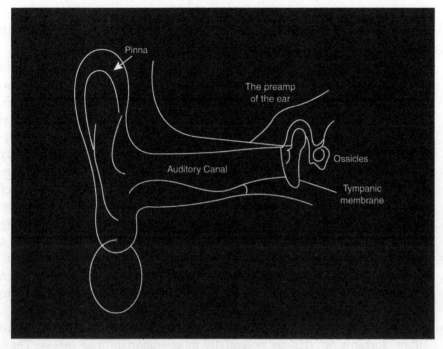

Figure 5.2 The inner ear

From this point, sound is relayed to the brain via nerves for processing, filtering and understanding. This relay is very quick because the ears are about as close to the brain as you can get. Very fortunate, as we rely upon our ability to process sounds quickly as a part of our survival instinct. Our ears are a 24/7 link between our minds and the outside world. They allow our brains to constantly monitor our surroundings and check for strange sounds that could mean peril.

My wife Sara was lying in bed one night when I was at my weekly poker school. She was asleep and dreaming, when her dreams took a strange turn and she was aware of a fountain appearing in an inappropriate place. Her unconscious mind was being spoken to by her conscious mind and it was trying to tell her that something was wrong and that she should not be enjoying the sound of gushing water. As it turned out, there was a flood upstairs and water was gushing through the ceiling of the front hall. Sara's conscious mind, alerted by her ears, woke her from her sleep because she was in some peril.

Every place where we sleep has its own sounds and the first few nights in any new room are always fitful as we are hearing new sounds that need to be taken seriously as potential threats. After we get used to them, however, we can sleep easily again, safe in the knowledge that our ears will let us know if there are any new sounds of which we should be aware.

The brain is incredibly good at recognizing sounds. We can differentiate between frequency jumps of 1 Hz in a range of almost 20,000. We can also hear many different sounds at once and switch our listening between them. This is the phenomenon that happened to me in Capri. I was listening to one thing but because I was still hearing everything around me, when a familiar sound came along it grabbed my attention and forced me to switch my focus. The same thing happens every day in thousands of different situations. If you are talking to a colleague and somebody on the other side of the room says your name, even if it is no louder than the conversation you are in, you will most likely turn and investigate why your name is being mentioned. When driving in a car, you may be on the phone, talking to a passenger or listening to the radio. There are many sounds around you, including the engine and the wind and road noise. If you hear a siren, even if it is faint and in the distance, then you will switch all your listening to concentrate upon locating the source.

We are naturally programmed to recognize that certain sounds, like sirens, screams or cries are potentially more important than others. Thus, when we hear them, we immediately switch from whatever we were previously listening to and pay them more attention. In extreme cases, the sounds of peril will trigger chemical reactions within our brains and bodies known as 'fight or flight'. This is primarily a burst of adrenaline that changes how we act and react. It can be triggered just by a little sound, such as a rattlesnake or the snap of a twig underfoot.

We can programme ourselves to recognize and pay attention to certain other sounds that have nothing to do with peril or survival. Hearing our names gets our attention, as do sounds that we associate with pleasure or some other benefit. If I hear the theme tune to *Seinfeld*, for example, I stop whatever I am doing to go and watch TV. My reaction to *Seinfeld* is not a pre-programmed survival instinct and yet it is as strong for me as the unconscious reaction to a siren or a scream. This indicates that we can learn to use different sounds as triggers for switching. This was recognized a long time ago by television programme makers, who use their theme tunes to grab attention before the show starts. It is a technique also employed by such historical figures as English town criers who would variously bellow three times 'hear ye' or some such call, before making their main announcements. This gave the townsfolk time to switch their listening, stop what they were doing and pay attention to important news.

Thus, sound is a call to action for the brain. We inherently understand that certain sounds or new sounds can mean that we are in peril and these sounds will grab our attention and may even create the fight or flight reaction. The relationship between sounds or voices and our brains is relatively straight-forward. It tends to be one of trying to understand the world around us. Sounds give our brains clues as to what is happening and our brains react by either ignoring the sounds if they are familiar and safe, or paying them attention if they are either unsafe or familiar and associated with a benefit.

Sonic branding certainly seeks to harness this relationship and use sound as a call to action. The Intel sonic logo does this, as do other famous sonic logos such as Direct Line insurance and Yahoo. Similarly, the *Seinfeld* or *The Simpson's* theme music work as calls to action that snatch our listening attention from wherever it was and place it firmly where the programme makers want it to be.

There is more to music, however, than the call to action. The relationship between the brain, the body and music is incredibly complex. If we are to call upon expert opinion, there can be few so well qualified as Charles Darwin, below paraphrased by Edmund Gurney, to start to explain what music means to humans:

> The suspicion does not appear improbable that the progenitors of man, either the males or the females, or both sexes, before they had acquired the power of expressing their mutual love in articulate language, endeavoured to charm each other with musical notes and rhythm. The impassioned orator, bard or musician, when with his various times and cadences he excites the strongest emotions in his hearers, little suspects that he uses the same means by which, at an extremely remote period, his half-human ancestors aroused each other's ardent passions during their mutual courtship and rivalry.[1]

So, Darwin tells us that the origins of music are ancient and tied up in passion, emotions and arousal. Many of the great thinkers agree with him and a trawl through any book of quotations will uncover how much thought has been given to music throughout the ages from the ancient Greeks to modern rock stars.

There are so many quotes regarding music and the way it has moved the greatest of people that the human evidence for its special powers is overwhelming but it is still useful, no matter how strong one's gut feelings maybe, to examine more scientific evidence for how music affects us.

Various scientific experiments have been carried out through the years on the nature of arousal and the role music can play. Instruments designed to observe and record the brain's electrical activity such as the electro-encephalogram, have been used to prove beyond doubt that music creates physiological arousal in people. The nature of the arousal observed ranges from changes in the pattern of brainwaves to pupil dilation, changes in respiratory rates and in the skin's electrical resistance (essentially a measure of sweat). Music has also been shown to create changes in muscle tensions. Experiments using an electro-myograph have shown significant changes in the amount of electrical activity in muscles during exposure to music. The next time you hear a tune and stamp your feet, recognize that this is not a wholly conscious activity. Most of it is rooted in the subconscious and the physiological.

In an interesting experiment on the conductor Herbert von Karajan, his pulse rate was recorded while he worked. His pulse rate was shown to increase most significantly at points in the music where he felt most moved rather than where he was waving his arms about the most. This is taken as clear evidence of the arousal abilities of music.

In studies conducted on children by the eminent psychologist Roger Brown, it was found that children exposed to new pieces of music that they had never heard before, reacted uniformly to the emotional content of the music, be it happy, sad or aggressive. He provided scientific evidence for the existence of musical devices and archetypes that make us a feel a certain way, regardless of the context, our mood or any prior associations. Anecdotally, we know this anyway. Any group of people listening, for example, to the opening passages of the *Jaws* theme by John Williams will feel the emotion of fear. It is composed according to archetype.

This is very good news for sonic branding. It means we can call upon the collective unconscious and design emotional messages. In much the same way as the Bauhaus pointed to a natural relationship between emotion, colour and shape – the dynamic yellow triangle, serene blue circle and static red square – so we can point to similar relationships in melody, harmony and instrumentation.

The ability to engage in emotional engineering is of the essence of branding and is the second reason, along with the call to action, why music is potentially the most powerful branding tool we have. To elevate music and sound above graphics or visuals as brand communicators could be seen as controversial. It is clear, however, that music or sonic stimuli have the ability to move or arouse us more quickly and more deeply than visual stimulus. A picture of a woman laughing may bring a smile to our faces but if we hear that woman's laughter we will probably laugh too. The opposite is even stronger. Pictures of war can be disturbing but to hear the screams and the explosions is far more powerful.

Which is the more arousing experience, an art gallery or a concert? Judging by the reactions of the patrons, we can safely say that the concert is more arousing. The last time I was at the Tate, I saw few people swaying side to side holding cigarette lighters above their heads. This seems to happen all the time at Barry Manilow concerts. As a pianist, Manilow knows all about arousal through music. As an entertainer, he also uses words and song lyrics to get his audiences going. The way that these different stimuli affect the brain has also been studied scientifically.

Experiments using electro-encephalograms to measure activity in the hemispheres of the brain have shown us that the left and right hemispheres have different processing roles. Similarly, observations of those with damage to their left or right brain hemispheres have shown us that verbal language and music are processed on opposite sides of the brain. Though there is rarely an absolutely clear demarcation between the functions of each hemisphere, these findings tally with what we already know about the 'personality' of each side of the brain.

LEFT BRAIN	RIGHT BRAIN
Logical	Random
Sequential	Intuitive
Rational	Holistic
Analysis	Synthesizes
Objective	Subjective
Parts	Wholes

Figure 5.3   Left and right brain attributes

Words are very left brain. We process them to find out what they mean and also construct sentences of them to express how we feel. This is a logical process that is quite removed from our emotions. If words and emotions were directly linked, we would never be tongue-tied in a tricky situation. The right brain, which is the emotional side, is where music is understood. There are many instances where people whose left brain has been damaged have still been excellent musicians. Vissarion Shebalin, a famed Soviet composer, suffered a stroke that rendered him unable to speak and yet he composed a fifth symphony.

Some sounds contain both words and music. Songs are processed and understood in the right, emotional hemisphere. Wherever words become associated with a melody, they become understood for their sound rather than for their rational meaning. Through processing and storage in the right hemisphere, the lyrics to a song become incredibly memorable. The left hemisphere remembers the meanings of words and can construct sentences but the right hemisphere remembers the order of the words in a song and can recall them exactly. The same phenomenon occurs with rhyming or rhythmic passages. They are also processed and stored in the right hemisphere. This is the reason why jingles and slogans that have a musical intonation become stuck in our memories long after their useful time has gone.

There are some very good reasons why music has to be memorable. Quite simply, until the middle of the last millennium, mankind had no way to record music. If you wanted to keep a song alive, you could not buy it and put it in a rack, you had to memorize it. As music has always been valued by society, we evolved the ability to remember music. It is known, through archaeological findings, that man has been making music for many, many thousands of years. In fact, every culture on the planet (assuming they have all now been identified) uses music in some way.

Flutes made from bone, dating from the Lower Palaeolithic period (around 30,000 BC) have been found in caves in southern France, the Pyrenees and parts of Russia. In construction, they were at the leading edge of the technology of the day, just as music software today is said to be even more advanced than that used by NASA. The cave paintings that have been found in these same caves are art, largely intact and retaining their original meaning. The figures depicted are often dancing, presumably to music but though we have found flutes, we have no idea what the music itself, the art-form, sounded like. It is possible, of course, that the paintings may themselves have been musical notation. Even if they were, we may never find out the tunes that used to get people on their feet and dancing.

Thus, music was handed down through the generations aurally, which meant that it had to be remembered. In this way, humans developed their musical memories beyond their memories for visual communications. The aural tradition of music is still around today. Aborigine tribes in Australia are known to create songs that relate directly to the lands that they occupy. Melodies rise and fall for hills and valleys. These songs, which serve an important purpose in the territorial society, are unwritten in a formal sense though they are, obviously, written in the land.

Ancient human musicianship is clearly not quite as ancient as musicianship from some of the earth's other great composers. Birds are thought to be the descendants of dinosaurs. They have been around for quite a long time and some of them sing beautifully. Birds are one of the very few animals who have brain lateralization in much the same way as the human left/right brain split. They are the most obviously musical of all the animals and the more we listen to them, the more compelling their musical credentials.

Luis Baptista, curator of ornithology and mammology at the California Academy of Sciences in San Francisco has identified that one of the most famous phrases in music, the opening 'da da da dummm' of Beethoven's 'Fifth Symphony' is actually a composition of the Mexican white-breasted wood wren. This is not to say that Beethoven actually heard the wood wren. Much more interestingly than that, it points to a collective unconscious shared between humans and the natural world. The evidence points to the existence of musical archetypes that could elicit similar responses in all humans. Such archetypes could be incredibly powerful for the communication of ideas and values. Mozart kept a starling as a pet and musical companion. Starlings teach their young to sing and are great mimics of what they hear. Mozart's starling gets a credit for the last movement of the 'Piano Concerto in G major'. The bird is said to have mimicked a phrase but turned the sharps to flats, impressing the composer. Beethoven too is thought to have plagiarized the European blackbird for the opening of his 'Violin Concerto in D, Opus 61'.

Starlings and blackbirds use their music for a most Darwinian purpose – finding a mate. The longer and more complex their song the better the sexual rewards. With Mozart's coaching, his starling must have been a real hit with the 'starlingettes'. This is not to say that birdsong is only legitimized when copied by humans. On the contrary, what this allows us to see is that music is interwoven with nature as well as human society and if we seek inspiration we can look to the sounds of nature as well as referencing the great classical composers. Overall, the knowledge being gained by science in this field serves more to enhance the reputations of the animals and put human endeavour into context.

Another notable group of nature's musicians is the whales, whom we know now to be extremely musical. Almost all whales sing but male humpbacks are thought to be the most tuneful, as they can sing for over 24 hours during the mating season cruise. Furthermore, according to Roger Payne of the Ocean Alliance in Massachusetts, who has been listening for more than 30 years, whales use rhythm and phrasing to create songs and what we might recognize as symphonic movements.

All of this further points to a collective unconscious for music, where the structures of the art are understood by many of the earth's species. For now however, we are only really interested in branding goods for human consumption so it is only the collective unconscious for music in humans that we need to remember.

The almond of emotion

The most recent research into the human responses to fear or peril stimuli has been carried out by Joseph LeDoux of New York University. His studies show that it is a special part of the brain called the amygdala (named from the Latin for its almond-like shape) that controls emotional, physiological response. The amygdala is positioned at the base of the two hemispheres of the brain and is thought to be the oldest and most developed part of the brain. It is hard-wired into the brain's circuitry and can react and respond to events such as a gunshot or a snake's rattle without the need for conscious thought. This makes its reaction our first reaction and in some way explains why we sometimes act irrationally in all kinds of situation.

It also plays a part in memory, specifically emotional and physiological memory. For example, if you are bitten by a cat, the next few times you see a cat, you will remember the events and other logical information that led up to the event; perhaps including what you were wearing and who you were with. These memories are thought to be stored in various areas of the two hemispheres of the brain. In addition to memories of rational information, seeing the cat will cause you to experience unconscious, physiological memories that may make your pulse race or bring out a sweat. These are thought to be controlled by the amygdala as would be similar emotional memories associated with music. Perhaps this explains why the listener might cry when hearing a sad piece of music from their past.

Dr Manfred Clynes, a neuroscientist, concert pianist and author of the music-making software SuperConductor, certainly agrees that music is strongly associated with emotions and memories. 'Music acts on the nervous system like a key in a lock, activating brain processes with corresponding emotional reactions.'[2] As far back as 1980, research into responses to music concluded that there is an emotional 'thrill' associated with listening that concurs with Clynes' assertion. The physiological cause of this was thought to be the endogenous (from within) production of beta-endorphins during listening to music, a phenomenon that has also lead to music being used in the treatment of pain associated with cancer.

The Mozart Effect, as identified by Don Campbell of the Institute of Music, Health and Education, points to the ability of music, Mozart in particular, to enhance mood and memory. Research carried out at the University of California at Irvine (UCI) demonstrated that Mozart's 'Piano Sonata for Two Pianos' was especially effective at improving the spatial learning skills of undergraduates, who showed an improvement of 8–9% in test scores after listening to just ten minutes of Mozart.

Intriguingly, associated research has shown that other types of music such as heavy metal and rap have an opposite effect upon the listener. An informal study of teenagers in southern California indicated that simple mental tasks became harder to perform under the influence of these genres compared to Mozart or even no music at all.

CHAPTER 6

The three elements of sound

If we were to treat every sound in the world separately then this book would be a little on the large side. There are millions of sounds out there that human beings can perceive and differentiate between. It is more useful for this book to put different types of sounds into categories so that we can make some general points that relate directly to our subject.

It is received wisdom within the sonic branding business, that there are three different types, or elements, of sound. These are voice, ambience (or effects) and music. This is an incredibly broad way of classifying the millions of different sounds that we hear during our lives. Broad as it is, however, I am yet to find a sound that could not be classified in this way. That said, I find it useful to treat these three areas slightly differently, as each has a different role regarding life in general and sonic branding in particular.

Voice

In sonic branding terms, voice relates to any sound produced by human beings as a result of air being forced from the lungs, through the voice box or larynx. This means that anything from a baby crying to Pavarotti singing can be counted as voice, as can the spoken word. The voice has a few very important roles. As humans, we use our voices to say words, which are rational, left-brain things that are the building blocks of language. The selection and consistent use of voice is an increasingly important area of sonic branding. So much is now communicated through recorded speech, not just via advertising but on IVRs and telephone hold systems, that the nature of the spokesperson becomes highly relevant to how messages are perceived.

In Chapter 22, we will examine through a detailed case study how Orange, with the help of Engine, a London-based creative strategy agency, has taken a great deal of care over their choice of voices for their expanding range of IVRs. We will also delve, in Chapter 18, into the advertising strategy of BMW (GB), who have found that the right voice, consistently used, can have great benefits for effective use of media. In this section, however, we will focus upon the role of singing in culture and further inform our understanding of how this key element of sound communicates to the listener.

Singing is a fundamental mode of human expression that has been practised by every culture in every age. Through song, every voice is capable of expressing distinct, recognizable and personal emotional messages that, due to the presence of words in almost all song, also convey the rational information of speech. This makes singing a very powerful human communicator, which is why it has dominated our culture for hundreds of years.

The first famous singers on record, so to speak, were the troubadours and trouveres of the eleventh through to the thirteenth centuries. Their talents were as storyteller, poet, composer and singer. Their function was to spread culture through their travels and songs and as singers unrelated to the church, they were the truest ancestors to modern-day popstars. They were all men, for women were not encouraged to sing until the late sixteenth century. Even then, there were no famous female singers, only talented courtesans whose contributions to the art were not officially recognized. The world of song was sexist but women got revenge upon men in a very strange way.

The church musicians of the day, particularly those around Rome and the Vatican, heard women singing and realized that musically, there was much to be said for the high vocal register. They wanted it for the church choirs but, obviously, the church could not allow women in the choir. The solution was to castrate men, thus causing their voices to become high pitch. The Castrato made the ultimate sacrifice for his music, right up until the end of the nineteenth century, and women of every age can only marvel at how stupid men were (are).

Singing developed throughout the period from 1500 to 1900 through the opera and operetta. With live performance as the only outlet for the singer, great emphasis was placed upon the technique of singing, particularly on projection, the art of being heard. Thus, the classical style was refined over the centuries and it can still be heard in today's great operatic singers.

The twentieth century, however, brought electrical amplification, recorded music and the radio. All of these had a great influence upon singing and allowed the many and varied styles we hear in popular music. Bob Dylan would have been nothing had he been trying to make a career as a singer 50 years previously but he and countless others benefited from the freedom from training and technique that microphones brought about. That said, in one major way the new technology brought a different type of constriction. As mentioned earlier, radio transmitters, speakers and crystals in the receivers were sensitive things back in the 1920s and led to the development of a safe, moderate singing style called 'crooning' that saved equipment from blowing up. A major consequence of the technological limitations was that one singer ended up sounding very much like another. Only a small number, Bing Crosby and Frank Sinatra among them, were able to really create their own sound. Since those days, however, the development of singing has been all about self-expression. The great song stylists from Billie Holiday to Nat King Cole, Elvis, Aretha and Bowie have all brought their own personality to the song and have emphasized the need for individuals to sound individual.

The drive for distinctiveness and self-expression is one that mirrors almost every aspect of life in the twenty-first century and serves as a lesson for brands to find their own voice. In Chapter 22, we will examine the branding implications of voice, both sung and spoken. We will discuss how different vocal qualities can be used to reflect brand values and consider some important case studies where the consistent use of a well-chosen brand voice has had a positive impact upon brand identity and experience.

Ambience

Some dictionaries tell us that voice is common to all vertebrates but for sonic branding, the noises that mammals make with their larynx or birds with their syrinx are classified as ambience. As such, they fall into a huge category of sounds that are heard every day in every environment. Ambient sounds include weather sounds, machine sounds and any sound that is not made by a human voice or by a recognizable musical instrument. Their role in sonic branding varies. Ambient sounds can form an important part of a sonic logo, as with that for the UK insurance broker Elephant, which uses an elephant's call, mixed with African drumming. They have been used to great musical effect in the Intel sonic logo, the notes of which are played using samples of ambient sounds mixed with melodic percussion. Perhaps their greatest potential role is in the design of sonic branding for environments, where natural sounds such as wind, rain or the sea can be used to create feelings of tranquil well-being in offices or waiting rooms.

The art of ambient sound developed originally with the theatre.[1] It is known that sound effects were employed in ancient Greek theatre and there are descriptions of lead balls being bounced on leather drum skins to produce the sound of thunder. Shakespearean theatre also rose to the challenge of thunder, rolling cannon balls down wooden troughs onto huge drums. The importance of thunder to sound effects continued to inspire theatre people into the eighteenth century. In 1708, John Dennis invented a new thunder-making method that employed the shaking of large copper sheets. The play in which these sounds debuted was a flop. The sound effect, however, was a great success. So much so, that other dramatists employed Dennis' techniques, literally 'stealing his thunder'. Believe it or not, this is the origin of this phrase.

Another linguistic nugget that the art of sound effects has given us is the term 'slapstick' for a genre of knockabout comedy. The slapstick was a device for making a sound like a whip crack that would accompany the pratfalls and eye pokes of comedy and variety shows of the early twentieth century. Slapstick as comedy was never more expertly done than in the cartoons and it was in the great cartoons of Warner Bros – Tom and Jerry, Roadrunner and Bugs Bunny, to name a few – that generations learned exactly what a 'splat', 'boing' or 'biff' sounds like. Sound effects, together with music, were integral to the appeal of cartoons and continue to be so. Often they provide far more than slapstick sounds, making up for a lack of dialogue in conveying the emotions of the characters and situations.

Before the great Hollywood cartoons came along, sound effects had undergone a fair amount of evolution since Dennis' thunder. The growth of live theatre had continued throughout the eighteenth and nineteenth centuries to a point where music hall and Vaudeville were popular, mass entertainment. The light-hearted nature of most variety shows leant itself to the use of humorous sound effects that could enhance the audience experience. As a result, theatres employed percussionists who used their ingenuity to create amusing or unusual sounds. The contraptions they used ranged from cowbells to wood blocks, ratchets, whistles and the aforementioned slapsticks. These were played live and in many cases were used to indicate when in the play an audience should laugh. The technique can still be heard today, where TV comedians will ask their drummer to play a 'dadum dah' when they have told a joke, usually in an ironic, post-modern way but an old technique nonetheless.

The same effects percussionists, also called utility men in the US (they were always male, apparently), were later employed by cinemas to accompany silent movies, together with house musicians. They plied their trade all over the world. In Japanese cinemas, they were called 'benshis' and they provided the sound effects for silent movies as well as voicing all the characters. Some benshis became stars in their own right, far outshining the silent films they accompanied, through their characterization. Utility men found their way from silent movie-theatres onto the radio in the 1920s and really transformed radio drama. The effects added realism and drama in a way that dialogue alone could not. Before radio embraced sound effects, actors would say lines like 'Who could that be knocking on the door?' while the audience at home heard no such knocking.

Ora and Arthur Nichols were two pioneers of live radio sound effects. They produced large contraptions capable of producing many different sound effects at the pull of a lever. Along with other contraptions such as mini doors and doorframes, rain sticks and splash tanks, they and other sound effects artists sought to recreate the sounds of the real world in the studio. These 'simulated' sounds were not universally acceptable, however, and some radio directors, Orson Welles notable among them, insisted on the real thing. On one famous show, set in the desert, he insisted that the actors walk on sand and had the studio floor covered in the stuff. He turned the microphones up so loud in order to capture the sounds, though, that the actors' voices overloaded the mics and he had to turn to sound effects artists and boxes of sand.

The sound effects art as we know it today was developed to overcome the limitations of 'simulated' effects, which were never absolutely accurate and tended to be used and re-used for every occasion. If there was a door to be slammed in the radio play, it sounded like every other door in every other radio play. It was the recording and manipulating of real sound, an art developed on both sides of the Atlantic from the 1930s onwards, that brought effects into the modern era. In the UK, sound effects were primarily developed by the BBC to add atmosphere to radio dramas. In the US, it was Hollywood that really embraced the art. The phonograph made the difference, providing a hardware platform for the sounds to be recorded live in the field and then brought to the studio for manipulation or playback. *King Kong*, in 1933, was a landmark movie for effects. The ape's roar was actually that of a lion, re-recorded at half-speed. Its chilling sound added to the great impact of the movie.[2]

A whole industry sprang up around recording and manipulating sound effects. The most famous exponent of the art was Jack Foley, a Hollywood effects man of the 1950s whose name has become the generic for sound effects work in the movies. Foley was one of the few people in the 1950s that could still do live sound effects, as opposed to applying them in post-production as popular from *King Kong* onwards. This made him the sound effects person most in demand during Hollywood's golden era and cemented his place in movie-making lore.

Today, huge sound effects libraries have been assembled in Hollywood and by the BBC in the UK. They are commercially available to anyone who can afford them and they are available in broadly two categories: ambient and spot sound effects. Ambient effects convey a background context or setting such as a rainforest or a car park. Spot effects convey an event such as a gunshot or a door bell.

There is much to be said, however, for 'do it yourself' sound effects. Whereas suitcases of equipment were needed in the 1930s to record sound, today a minidisc recorder and a little microphone will give great results. Indeed, technology continues to impact sound effects in every way, from ease of recording to the infinite variations that can be made to natural sounds using software algorithms. The role of the effects, however, remains the same. They add dramatic context and emotion to live and broadcast entertainments.

Music

> Writing about music is like dancing about architecture – it's really a stupid thing to want to do.
>
> Elvis Costello[3]

Trying to define music is always fun! This is what the *New Oxford Dictionary of English* has to say: 'The art or science of combining vocal or instrumental sounds (or both) to produce beauty of form, harmony and expression of emotion.' This is a fabulous definition and I am yet to find any other that puts it more succinctly. If it has a flaw, it is that music today incorporates ambient sounds that are neither vocal nor instrumental but I will overlook that because the basics are so good.

Music is the fundamental element of sound in terms of sonic branding. As well as the cultural reasons outlined already, there are many other important references in this book as to why music is so important for brands. Perhaps the simplest, though, is that music can incorporate any and all the sounds in the world. If we can record them they can be used in music, be they vocal, ambient or made by any of the thousands of musical instruments man has invented.

Music is a huge subject and many books have been written about its art, its social functions, its psychology and just about every other aspect of the cultural phenomenon. It touches the lives of everyone in some way and thanks to our ability to record it, has become one of the dominant art forms in western culture. It has also become the victim of its own success because as any true musician will tell you, the drive to create is artistic yet the driving forces of today's music are big business. Today there is a great feeling that music has been hijacked for the sole purpose of generating wealth and this is an accusation that has been levelled at the sonic branding industry as well as the more obviously culpable recording industry.

Hunter S. Thompson is often interpreted wildly and the following common misquote was originally written as a critique of the TV industry. Attributable or not, it resonates with many involved with the music industry: 'The music business is a cruel and shallow trench, a long plastic hallway where thieves and pimps run free and good men lie like dogs. There is also a negative side.'[4] The music industry has undoubtedly become a huge money-spinner and as befits any industry in our capitalist democracy, it is run for the sole purpose of profit. Unfortunately, the drive to lower costs and increase revenues does not seem to be wholly compatible with the way that great musicians and composers create great music. It may sound disingenuous coming from a person who makes their living through music as a commercial tool but I believe in the sanctity of the art and the great unquantifiable benefits to humanity of great music.

This is why Sonicbrand works with top-class composers and invests so much time in seeking out the best talent. We aim to provide the purest of emotional benefits to the stakeholders of our clients' brands – the enjoyment of good music. Along the way, we help brands express themselves and generate belief but we never lose sight of the fact that we do our clients the best service by creating great music for their identity and their communications.

We also remind ourselves that music existed long before brands and will exist long after them. The aim of sonic branding, in relation to music is not to pollute the art-form but to more accurately express the emotions of individual brands through fabulous music. In the same way that individual film scoring, rather than the use of 'fake books', allowed individual movies to truly express their own meanings, we wish to give brands that same freedom. If we do this, we will be helping brands to communicate and also leaving a legacy of great music that defines the era in which we live.

As Sting said at the 2001 Britannia Music Awards (Brits), 'Music is its own reward.' I agree with him and so do the many composers, producers, instrumentalists, sound designers and vocalists I have had the pleasure to have worked with.

Inside the composer's studio

GLOSSARY

Sampler: Records and recreates the sounds of 'real' instruments or effects, giving the opportunity for editing the sonic patterns to create new and interesting sounds.

Sequencer: The computer instrumentalist; the sequencer tells the sampler what sounds to play and when, a little like a one-man band with multiple instruments strapped to his body.

Audio: Not all instruments are digital. Any real sounds (voices or a violin, for example) that are recorded into the sequencer are called audio.

Outboard: Processing techniques for editing and altering the way audio sounds.

MIDI (Musical Instrument Digital Interface): The digital language by which sequencers, samplers and other digital instruments communicate with each other.

Technology has undoubtedly played a major role in the growth and scope of sonic branding. Much of the opportunity has been offered up by proliferation of the consumer's sonic devices such as mobile phones, PDAs PCs and radios. Perhaps of more immediate importance, though, have been the technological advances made in the composer's studio over the last 20 years. Quite simply, technology has revolutionized how music is made, the cost of the creative process and the scope for creativity of a single producer or composer.

Music has always been heavily influenced by technological innovation as successive generations have sought to create new instruments and new sounds using the cutting edge technology of the day. The drum was hi-tech many thousands of years ago. Five hundred years ago, early adopters had a harpsichord. In around 1740 technophiles simply had to have a piano. In 1841 it was the saxophone that grabbed attention and in the late twentieth century, the sampler and synthesizer became the must-have instruments for any contemporary musician.

Modern digital samplers, which represent sounds from every conceivable instrument, are probably the most important innovation in music since the invention of the piano with its great dynamic and emotional range. Digital samplers allow a single composer or producer, armed only with a computer-based sequencer, keyboard and mouse to play almost every known instrument, recording and manipulating their sounds note by note.

Thirty years ago, if a producer wanted a violin section to play on a recording, the only thing to do was to write out the arrangements on manuscript and hire a number of violinists to come and play their violins. Today, armed with an Apple Mac and a set of strings samples, the same composer, with practice, can play every violin themselves, straight onto a hard-drive at broadcast quality. Obviously, this has had an impact upon violinists as there are fewer gigs around today than ever before. It has also had beneficial effect of enabling the marvellous sounds of the world's instruments to be recreated expertly without the need of a lifetime's study and practice.

Samples have allowed music to diversify, bringing the sounds of the world into the musical vocabulary of every composer. Though samples have their limitations, their ability to open up a world of orchestration has been revolutionary and samplers are a major contributor to the possibilities of the composer working in sonic branding.

That said, the quality involved in hearing a real musician playing a real instrument will almost always make more satisfying music and where time or budget allow, we try to generate as much work for instrumentalists as possible.

Modern music technology, as well as enhancing the range of instruments, makes the process from conception to realization much quicker and cheaper than it has ever been before. It is now possible for one person to write and record an orchestral symphony with didgeridoo and Tibetan bowl soloists, from the comfort of their own home in a tiny fraction of the time that such a strange exercise would have taken 30 years ago. This means that talented composers with access to the right equipment can convey their musical ideas in sampled form working to deadlines that suit the fast-moving world of brands and advertising. Though more time is always better, composers can now work in the same time zone as the rest of us.

The same revolution that computers brought to graphic designers has been brought to composers, though the complexity of music has required a longer and more complex development process for the software. It is reckoned that most audio/MIDI sequencer and recording software systems are rivalled only by NASA software for their complexity. As a result, making music using software does need training but mastery of a digital orchestra can be gained in years, whereas it can take a lifetime to master a single instrument in the traditional realm.

Part one: conclusion

The three elements of sound give us an extremely large palette for sonic branding and technology gives us an almost limitless number of locations and media where the palette can be employed by a brand. Given the diversity of the opportunity, it is unsurprising that most brands are yet to approach their use of sound from a consistent brand perspective. The choices available are vast and the experience, information and research required to make the right choices are highly specialized. As a result, the vast majority of brands have a hotchpotch of sounds representing them. Approach almost any brand and you will discover that the sound for each touchpoint is completely different. Some of it is good and 'on-brand', some of it is bad and 'off-brand'. Our clients most often ask us how we approach the difficult issue of creating consistency across the many media channels and physical touchpoints of a brand.

The answer is simple. There may be 100 different media channels but people have only one set of ears. We think about the human beings that will hear our work rather than the medium and go from there. The essence of sonic branding is to generate consistency across touchpoints and give brands the creative and strategic knowledge to understand what their sonic branding does for their brand. We are all just waking up to the opportunity and finding out about the range of opportunities in the age of sonic touchpoints. In doing so, we are discovering new ways to reward stakeholders. Ultimately, we are building trust and belief through a fundamental emotional communicator that is the match for any other expression of a brand from a graphic logo to a scent.

Sound relates to almost every discipline in branding and has a role in the creation as well as the communication of brands. Sonicbrand uses music to help clients understand what their brands stand for before we help them define how their brands should sound. We can do this because sound and music in particular are universal languages of emotion.

The 'Intel in Capri' story started our journey but the relationship between sound and brands is much more interesting than that. Sound, as we have shown, is exciting and diverse. Branding is just as broad and needs to be understood before we can really evaluate the role of sound in context. In order to progress, then, we have to examine the true nature of brands, how they are created and where sonic fits into their world.

PART 2

The Nature of Brands

I have read many, many books about brands. Most of them had interesting prefaces and then sank into an unreadable mess of diagrams and theory. The aim of this next section is to tackle the tricky issue of what makes a brand without falling into the trap of believing that brands are scientific. As I set about learning about brands through reading and many discussions with brand experts, it became increasingly clear to me that despite my desire to be able to qualify and quantify them through mathematics, the truth is that brands are soft and fluffy. They are very complex, organic entities and in many instances the nearest parallel to how they grow and develop is to be found in the world of art. Art is hard to define and brands can be just as hard. This is bad news for the accountants and their balance sheets.

Despite the growth in the popularity of the word 'brand', it has proved very hard to find a pre-existing definition that means what I think it should mean. This is chiefly because the brand world is changing very rapidly and the truths about brands that held even a couple of years ago have been superseded. 'Brand' is an overused word and it has come to mean many different things in today's society. When I typed the word into the Google™ search engine I was given over 13,500,000 results. There are so many companies and individuals who care about brands, think about brands and work with brands that it is easy to understand why the meaning of the word is constantly shifting and why it has got a little bit of a bad reputation.

Brands do not deserve bad reputations but some of the people who exploit them do. Brands, in essence, are actually beautiful things, nearer as I have said to works of art than anything else. To explain why this is the case and why brands are worth your time and effort, I must take you on a journey into the minds of the experts and let you in on the wisdoms of twenty-first century branding.

CHAPTER 7

A historical perspective

We will start with a couple of traditional definitions of a brand. First, 'an identifying mark burnt on livestock'; and second, just as prosaically 'a type of product manufactured by a particular company under a particular name'.[1] I work with many brands but the last time I checked I was working with no cows' arses. Therefore, interesting as the history of domestic cattle may be, I think we can ignore the first definition and go straight on to the second, that a brand is a type of product manufactured under a particular name.

This definition certainly tallies with what is thought to be the world's first brand. In c. 200 BC a Syrian sandal maker marked his sandals with his name and opened up a whole kettle of fish. The first brand was marked only with the maker's name. Every subsequent brand has also been marked with a name. Names are absolutely fundamental to brands, always have been, always will be. Names are also fundamental to humanity. Talmudic scholars tell us that something cannot exist until it has a name and that a name is fundamental to the essence of a being. In fact, the name of God is taken to be so important, that it is not meant to be spoken aloud. This is heavy, spiritual stuff, however, so if you want to know more, check out the Talmud. Suffice to say, it is an ancient Hebrew text that contains the foundations for much of the moral law of the western world. It has a lot to say about pretty much everything and were it to address the subject of brands, it would tell us that they need denominations.

The strongest brands today started out in the late nineteenth century with just their good names. Brands like Kellogg's, Coca-Cola and Marmite showed then, and show us today, that the right name has always been fundamental to the success of a brand. In terms of communication and marketing, these goods only needed a name because the products themselves were genuinely different or superior to goods that had gone before. The products were unique without having to consciously engineer a unique selling point. Quite simply, all they had to do to stand out in the grocery shops was have a label that stated their name and thus differentiated them from the generics.

The growth of these brands shaped understanding of what constituted a brand and for some time, a definition of a brand as a named good held sway. If all the other cereals are sold out of bags labelled as 'corn' or 'barley', then a box with Kellogg's written on it will clearly stand out; so the name-based definition was still accurate 120 years ago. The world's view of brands has changed somewhat more in the last 120 years than it did over the preceding 2,000. For a start, there are more brands around these days and differentiation means working a little harder than just having a name. Names are still important but today we understand that there are other factors that define a brand.

First, we have to acknowledge, unlike the *Oxford English Dictionary* (OED), that brands are not just products. Just about anything can be a brand these days. This includes the traditional commercial products or services, a social movement such as a charity, religious bodies such as the Anglican Church, political parties (see New Labour) or even just a person.

New Labour

New Labour won its first general election in the United Kingdom on 1 May 1997. The New Labour majority of 179 was the biggest ever held by the Labour Party and represented a landslide victory over the old enemy, the Conservatives, who had been beset by allegations of 'sleaze' and had seemingly become complacent after 18 years in power.

The reason that the Conservatives had held power for so long, despite some unpopular policies and personalities, was that the electorate had stopped trusting the Labour Party, the official opposition, back in the late 1970s. How then, did the Labour Party win back the trust of the people and win the 1997 general election?

1997 was the first great victory for the brand-led political party in the UK. It was a triumph as much for branding techniques as it was for policy. In fact, much of the policy that New Labour proposed was 'business as usual'. In ideological terms, they offered very little that was different to the Conservatives but they managed to win the hearts, minds and trust of the population of the UK by other means. They did this by focusing on their brand and delivering an absolutely consistent message to the people.

First, they called themselves New Labour. A new name for a new party. This made a clear statement to the electorate that this was a party removed from the unsuccessful and unloved Labour party of the 1970s.

New Labour had a lovely logo. The Labour Rose was visible everywhere that Labour spokespeople were. It had been created for the election and it resonated with the *Daily Mail*-reading, middle-class English who had traditionally been at the heart of the Conservative constituency.

A consistent font was employed and the new Labour red was visible in all the literature and at all the events. It was usually the colour of choice for Tony Blair's ties but not always. A calming, traditional blue tie was also in the New Labour colour palette.

New Labour used a new language full of positive words and rhetoric and only a select few were permitted to speak on behalf of the party. Previously noisy Labour voices such as Gerald Kaufman's became silent in the run-up to the election as consistent words were consistently delivered by the same spokespeople.

As icing on the branding cake, New Labour used music. It took D-Ream's anthemic 'Things Can Only Get Better' and turned it into a New Labour brand property. Perhaps more than anything else that New Labour did to differentiate itself from old Labour, it was this. Previous generations of Labour supporters had rallied to the chorus of 'The Red Flag', a left-wing favourite. 'Things Can Only Get Better' was young, trendy in a New Labour way and full of positive language and emotions. Most importantly, it really resonated with the imaginations of the electorate. It was great sonic branding and an inspiration to us all. Unfortunately, it lived its useful life and can never be used again by the party as the lyrics would do them no favours as an incumbent government.

Peter Montoya and Tim Vandehay of Millennium Advertising, California, contend that individual people are brands. They outline their arguments and give branding advice in their book *The Personal Branding Phenomenon*.[2] Through a series of case studies, all of them originating from the United States, as would be expected, they show how branding techniques have been employed by superstars such as Oprah Winfrey and Michael Jordan. They conclude that anyone can enhance their personal brand to achieve greater success.

Undoubtedly, they are right to conclude that people can be brands. Elvis, Madonna and Kylie all have logos, value sets and business models that set them out as brands. In fact, the cult of celebrity and personality that has been taking hold of the *Hello!* and *Heat* generation in recent years in the United Kingdom, with an even longer history in the United States, lends more credence to the idea of people as brands than even Montoya and Vandehay.

CHAPTER 8

Brand and its symbols

Way back in the dark ages of 1960, the American Marketing Association (AMA) put forward a definition of a brand that is interesting to note. They describe it as: 'A name, term, symbol or design, or a combination of them, intended to identify the goods or services of one seller or group of sellers and to differentiate them from those of competitors'.[1]

This definition was one of the first 'official' definitions to see that symbols or designs were important to brands, though in reality, symbols and designs had been used to identify entities for many thousands of years by this stage. For reference, read the Old Testament and consider symbols and designs used to differentiate Judaism from other ways of life. The Star of David, still the national symbol of Israel, was a favourite with the Hebrews from c. 2000 BC.

The AMA, however, were among the first trade bodies to let the cat out of the bag. They formally admitted to the world that the great power of symbols and designs that had long been harnessed by nations and religions could be used by those wishing to sell goods or services. Before we give credit to a trade association, however, we should give credit to the guy who was going around telling everyone about the power of symbols at the time. His name Carl Jung; he pretty much invented analytical psychology and was, without doubt, one of mankind's greatest thinkers. His life's work was full of analysis of symbolism and he finally defined them for the general populous, rather than for his fellow psychologists, in his final and most accessible text *Man and His Symbols*. To paraphrase, he defined a symbol as a term, a name or an image that contains specific associations in addition to its obvious everyday meaning.[2] A symbol is different to a sign, which is always less than the concept it represents, because a symbol always stands for more than its obvious meaning. The reason why symbols were and are employed by people is that they can be used to represent ideas that are beyond words. For example, a picture of a dove may be used as a symbol of peace – a very large concept represented by a small picture.

Jung had been banging on about symbols for many years and the marketing fraternity had been well aware of the relevance of the emerging knowledge of psychology all the way back to the 1920s, when Sigmund Freud's assertions were taken as the basis for the public relations (PR) industry. Just as Freud's nephew, Edward Bernays, put in place the central philosophies of PR, based upon Freud's assertions of the secret desires of humans, so Jung's understandings were adopted by visionaries who sought to put symbols and design at the centre of how brands were defined in the twentieth century.

Walter Landor was a German who studied art in London before moving, very sensibly, to San Francisco, California, around the time of World War II. As a student of the Bauhaus movement, he was well schooled in the idea that colour and shape, through their direct relationships, were fundamental human communicators. As such, he knew that those wishing to sell goods and services could harness their power. He also recognized that business was the patron with the deepest pockets and that working in the commercial world would give his designs the maximum possible audience.

Post-depression USA was the perfect place for Landor to start to practise his skills. He helped lift the mood with his designs and colours, quickly building a reputation for designing the graphic identities for famous brands of the time such as S&W Fine Foods. Though he was definitely not the first to do this, he was one of the best publicists of the discipline and the company that bares his name thrives today. Landor supplemented what he had learned from the Bauhaus movement with what he saw around him. He noticed how good graphic design had a lasting and beneficial effect on those wishing to sell goods and services and he noticed, no doubt, how the opposite was true.

One of the first modern brands, Kodak, had been using smart graphic design since the late 1800s (the logo has changed little in over 100 years). The founder of Kodak, George Eastman, was a pioneering photographer and used his trained eye to build his own brand using designed text and graphics. He may well be the father of modern brands but it is amazing that it took 2,000 years between the Syrian sandal maker and Eastman for graphic design to really take hold in branding. One reason why it took so long for this to happen was the slow pace of technology. Printing pictures did not become a common or cost-effective activity until the late 1800s and it was only when the new technology was opened up to businessmen like Eastman that they could use it to sell their goods and services. (In an interesting parallel, it is worth noting that cheap technology for recording and reproducing sound has only become available in the last ten years, giving a much broader access to the creation and playback of music.)

Once graphics were possible, however, a brand-wagon formed and it was lead by the fast moving consumer good (FMCG). FMCG brands really went overboard on design from the late 1800s onwards. This came to a head in the 1920s by which time logos, pictures and packaging design were fundamental to brands that were, in a functional sense, homogeneous. The FMCG sector at the time was one of the few truly competitive markets and the purpose of design was (and remains) differentiation.

In the UK and the US, road and rail transport had slowly brought a mobility of distribution to goods that were packaged with long sell-by dates (not that the sell-by date existed at that stage, just that anything in a can or jar was deemed to last forever). In the UK, Robertson's and Hartley's, among many others, distributed marmalades and jams nation-wide in jars; Persil, Surf and Sunlight created and distributed their washing powders and soaps all over the country with the promise that whites would be whiter. These goods were shipped out to compete with the local jam and soap makers as well as the other branded goods of the time. Once in the local shops, they needed to differentiate themselves not only from generic commodities but from each other. A name was no longer enough and logo designs, together with package designs for the new goods, gave an air of quality and a guarantee of standards to the housewife (sexist, I know).

The birth of mass media sonic branding

It was during the 1920s, that the use of sound as a marketing medium first came into public and corporate consciousness. The first commercial radio station, KDKA, was founded in 1920 by Frank Conrad, an employee of the Westinghouse company, a manufacturer and retailer of wirelesses. He and his employer had noticed that when they broadcast music, sales of the radio equipment they sold increased, so they applied for a licence, upped the juice on the transmitter and created a new commercial medium.

Conrad's activity was quickly copied by many other new radio station owners but while Conrad succeeded, over half the stations founded over the first five years of commercial radio closed down soon after. The overriding reason was that there was no proven revenue model, outside of equipment sales and a debate raged as to how to make money from radio. Options such as a licence fee, some method of subscription and encoding or philanthropy were considered and trialled with varying success. We do not have to look too hard to see many parallels between the troubled growth of radio in the 1920s and the growing pains of the Internet in the late 1990s.

Programming was created and broadcast largely to sell more radio sets and the commercial drive was to create content that appealed to as wide an audience as possible. Whether stations could make money or not, the common sense approach was to try to gather as many listeners as possible.

Commercial radio was actually seen as a public service in the early days but the transparent need for revenue soon saw commercial messages starting to dominate the medium. The speed with which this happened was astonishing, leading Herbert Hoover, the 31st president of the United States but then Secretary of Commerce, to bemoan at a radio industry conference in 1922 that: '[It would be] inconceivable that we should allow so great a possibility for service to be drowned in advertiser chatter.'[3]

Opinions such as these did not deter the FMCG manufacturers from seeking a way to use the communication power of sound to get their own messages across. They spotted an opportunity in all the people gathered, listening to the radio and in doing so gave stations programming budgets and new means of revenue generation. The way they did this was simple and enduring. They put together their own groups and paid for them to perform on the radio. The Royal Typewriter Salon Orchestra, the Lucky Strike Orchestra, Vick's Vap-o-rub Quartet, and the Cliquot Club Eskimos were all examples of this practice.

Beyond that, they started to sponsor programming and the 'soap opera' was born. These early US commercial radio sponsorships represent the first mass market use of what might very loosely be called sonic branding and helped reinforce the images of quality and heritage that the newly created names, logos and packaging conveyed.

It was during the 1920s that famous FMCG manufacturers invented the idea of 'brand management'. The knowledge associated with this concept was a competitive advantage and it took until the 1950s for the secrets to really get out into the broader public and corporate consciousness. Even when the man in the street did find out that brand management was essentially 'emotional engineering' and had been going on for decades, the public was only really aware that the instruments by which they were being manipulated were logos and names. Even today, few people realize how important other brand elements, such as music, are to the brand choices they make.

Over the 1920s and 1930s, the drive for symbols continued apace as printing became cheaper and the print media proliferated. By the 1940s, Walter Landor, who was obviously a smart man, was building a business in graphic design for brands. He took the common understanding that brands were primarily based upon graphic design and supplied to meet the demand; as a graphic designer he was perfectly suited to do so. For many years, and to this day, his company told the world that to have a brand meant to have some great symbol and associated designs. He went further too. No doubt partly to publicize himself and partly because it seemed a good idea at the time, he encouraged his clients to whack their new designs all over their products and service deliveries. Walter Landor is credited with one of the all-time great symbols, the Levis jeans logo. Designs like that one must have made a powerful case for the strategic arguments with which Landor augmented his symbols.

What made a more powerful argument was that Landor was intrinsically right – for the times. 1950s USA was booming with manufacturing and service innovations. In the same way that World War I had accelerated innovation in things like tinned food, World War II accelerated innovation in just about everything from automobiles to plastics. The US economy rode on the wave of manufacturing innovation and reflected it in an unprecedented amount of product design. This meant that the new products really did seem to be different and superior to those that had come out even a few months before.

If the product is noticeably different, the job of the brand or corporate identity (CI) as it was more commonly termed at the time, is simply to say who it is that makes it. This meant that Landor's agenda was perfect for the 1950s. All that was needed was a good name and a logo and the product itself made up the rest of the brand. Hence, the AMA's brand definition in 1960. This definition, having its roots in the 1890s was so widely publicized and believed that it dominated the world's brand thinking right up until the late 1990s. Thereby, for 100 years, the broad base of brand thinking pointed to names and graphic devices as being the essence of brands.

Another compelling argument for this approach was the development of the trademark system. The trademark, of course, is an easily understood entity that can be logged and protected. It also has a simple cost to it, that of design and registration. The trademark, in many ways, was seen as being the same as a brand. This is no surprise when you re-read the AMA's brand definition, which is actually a very good definition of a trademark. Today, we would define a trademark as 'a symbol, word or words, legally registered or established by use as representing a company or product'. Uncannily similar, you will agree, to the AMA's definition of a brand in 1960. In the years between 1960 and the late 1990s, an industry sprang up around the creation and registration of trademarks. This industry was directly related to the commercial graphic design businesses like Landor Associates and centred upon lawyers, who gave a further air of legitimacy to the idea that graphic design was the be all and end all of brands.

It is certainly true that trademarks are important to brands: they allow protection in the same way as copyright. Today, however, most experts understand that a trademark is not the essence of a brand but simply a potential part of a brand's identity. One very notable exception was shown in the

definition of a brand proposed in 2000 in *The Future of Brands*, a book by
Rita Clifton and Esther Maughan of the brand behemoth, Interbrand. It contended that a brand is: 'A mixture of tangible and intangible attributes, sym-
bolised in a trademark, which, if properly managed, creates influence and
generates value.'[4] Fair enough for a company that built its success creating
and registering names and trademarks but already out of date and at best
simplistic. Brands are symbolized in far more complex ways than just
trademarks and for Interbrand to contend otherwise is strange, given their
pre-eminence in the branding industry of the 1990s. The knowledge that can
be gained by studying the strongest brands of the post-war era, as defined
by Interbrand so well in their annual league tables, will lead us to a far more
interesting brand definition.

CHAPTER 9

McBrands

One brand, more than any other has shown us that trademarks and brands are different. This brand set the agenda for how we perceive brands today but it took 40 or more years for the lessons to filter through and even now, the branding industry is dominated by businesses that sell graphic design and trademarks ... but not for much longer. The brand that helped the world see that a name, design and trademark were just elements of a brand and not the essence of a brand was growing slowly and quietly at the same time and in the same place as Landor Associates. During the 1940s and 1950s, largely unknown to the marketing fraternity, a new, great brand was being born in the sunshine state of California. It too rode the economic boom of the post-war years but it and a few contemporaries were to set a new agenda for creating and defining brands.

McDonald's was founded by Richard and Maurice McDonald (no Ronald?) in 1937. Originally, they had escaped the Depression and the east, looking for gold in the movie business. Their talents as set builders allowed them to save the money needed to build a cinema but when that failed they turned their hands to making 'McDonald's Famous Burgers'. They opened a drive-in restaurant, the kind you might be familiar with from watching *Happy Days* or the opening titles to the classic *Flintstones* cartoons.

Kids in southern California loved to hang out at drive-ins. Here they were served cheap food late into the night by 'car hops', usually pretty girls in short skirts. The McDonald Brothers' Burger Bar Drive-In was the right business in the right place at the right time. California was flooded with investment from the federal government of the US, had the kind of year-round climate that was ideally suited to 'hanging out' and had an abundance of kids with cars and cash.

The McDonald brothers' success was considerable but nevertheless, they became disillusioned with the drive-in restaurant they had founded. There seemed to be too much bother serving customers in their cars, too much hassle finding short-order cooks and too many broken glasses to be replaced every night. So, they changed the way they did business. Though what they did owes much to the factory assembly line, I believe that their background in entertainment had an effect on the way they did it.

In short, they invented McDonald's as we know it. They pared the menu down to foods eaten without a knife and fork; they brought in the division of labour in preparation (one person for the burgers, one for the fires and so on); and they served everything in paper rather than on a plate or in a glass. They also decided to stop employing car hops, much to the disappointment no doubt, of every red-blooded teenage boy.

The next thing they did was also genius but incredibly simple. They decided they needed a new building for the restaurant. This one had to be visible from far away, so Richard McDonald designed it to have two neon-lit arches on its roof that looked like an *M* when viewed from a distance. With no training as a designer or architect, the Hollywood set-building brothers created an enduring theatre of hamburgers and possibly the most loved and reviled logo in the world.

That was not all, however, because they then introduced the Speedee Service System – a way for the staff to behave that described exactly what was expected of them. This became the value set for the whole company. They recruited staff to support their vision. They wanted a family clientele and experience told them that employing young female staff would mainly attract young men so rather than become a teen hangout, they only employed young men. In their total innovation of the restaurant concept, McDonald's effectively laid a blueprint for brands for the next half-century. They had a good name, they developed a great logo, serendipitously, some ten years after they set up, they recruited to support their ideas and they trained their staff to believe in the Speedee Service values.

These principles were copied, very quickly, by a huge number of competitors all over the US. The ideas and inspiration that took the brothers a lifetime to develop were copied by other people all over the nation but the McDonald brothers were not one-trick ponies. What continued to place McDonald's at the forefront of their industry was their belief in delivering a consistent product and service. They achieved this by implementing a rigorous regime, specifying the nature and method behind every burger, bun and soft drink. Everything about the restaurants was metred precisely, ensuring that the customer always got what the menu promised. More to the point, every customer got exactly what they expected and that was the key to building trust.

The food was not all that was specified. The architecture style that was introduced in the first restaurant was used as a pattern for subsequent restaurants and the lucky logo became a beacon to low-income families all over the country that had not been catered for previously by restaurants.

The interiors, too, were specified according to the brothers' exacting standards, but there was usually some design cue reserved for the location of the restaurant. If you think that the idea of global/local is new then just look at the range of McDonald's restaurant interiors world-wide.

McDonald's had consistent food, architecture and staff. They all supported the value set of Speedee Service. Furthermore, McDonald's had its own in-store music programme. It had uniform lighting, heating, flooring and just about everything else. As a result of its vast success throughout the late twentieth century, it has become a model for how brands behave today. In fact, the McDonald's model is the one adhered to by most of today's branding experts.

McDonald's was the first company to view the entire brand experience. Brand experience has become a buzz around the industry in the last two years. It refers to a brand philosophy prescribing that every time a customer comes into contact with a brand, no matter what the channel, the experience should be consistent with the central belief of the brand. Consistency increases the probability of reaching target customers effectively.[1]

It took the industry a long time to catch on to this view; in the meantime McDonald's has come to dominate the world of fast food. The secrets are now visible, however, exposed in *Fast Food Nation*, by E. Schlosser. Perhaps the most interesting revelation in that best-seller is a point that is easy to miss. In a quote from a McDonald's communications strategy meeting the following objective was identified. McDonald's wanted to 'make the customers believe that McDonald's [was] their "Trusted Friend" '.[2]

CHAPTER 10

The essence of brand is belief

Trust is a belief in reliability.[1]

What McDonald's did better than anyone else was to create belief among their customers that they were getting decent food at a good price and that the chain would always deliver the same portions in the same wrappers in the same type of environment. McDonald's promised all of this and when customers walked through the doors, this is exactly what they got.

McDonald's kept their promises and in doing so they became trusted as you or I would if we were to commit to something and then deliver. They were also very friendly. The brand spokesman was a clown, very unfunny but a familiar archetype that resonates all over the world as being friendly and unthreatening. The staff was trained, at least in the US, to be friendly too; politeness and courtesy were a part of the service. More than that, McDonald's had a strategy for hosting children's parties and generally looked after kids through happy meals, balloons and hats.

McDonald's brand was based upon a belief that the brothers had in their way of doing things. Their ideas were strong and their execution was consistent. They made promises and kept them and customers grew to believe in the brand as a trusted friend. If it were not for allegations of sharp practice and environmental harm, the brand would still be everyone's favourite, but more of that later.

The word belief came up time and again while researching this book. It certainly seems to be the case that today's brand experts put belief right at the heart of a brand. In September 2002, we asked Tania Mason, editor of the Branding section of *Marketing* magazine to give us her definition of a brand: she described it as a 'promise of standards'. This is very much in keeping with the McDonald's brand story and it is pretty easy to understand.

Tim Greenhill, Managing Director of Greenhill McCarron also asserts that brands are based upon beliefs, which must be commonly held by the staff and customers of an organization. Does this mean that logos and trademarks have no relevance to a definition of a brand post-McDonald's? Greenhill would argue that the traditional model of name and trademark are just as important as ever but today, not everyone is certain that brands, if they have belief, need logos.

The Times, in October 2002, ran a front page splash entitled 'Death of the Logo'.[2] The article was certainly not heralding the death of brands. The reference was to the current movement by fashion houses to completely rethink the logo and trademark. Gucci and Prada are at the top end in the world of fashion. They set the tone for everyone else and the trend they are currently setting, in a world post 11 September and the 'Battle of Seattle', has been to downsize or even in some cases completely remove the logos from their goods. In doing so, they are reflecting the times and may be defining how society will view logos for years to come.

This is not just another trend. It represents a growing feeling among those who work with brands that logos and symbols, which had come to be seen as a promise of standards, no longer mean as much as they once did, particularly in a world of counterfeiting. If the Gucci logo was a promise of standards but more Gucci bags on the street are counterfeit than real, then the promise is broken because part of the promise is exclusivity and self-expression. If anyone can have a Gucci fake, which can be of merchantable quality, then the Gucci logo is a broken promise.

The label has found a way to make a promise and keep it. It now relies more heavily on great design of unique features. Outside of Gucci, Christian Louboutin, the shoe designer, has taken to making his shoes with red soles. No doubt when he is copied, he will need to find a new way to differentiate his designs but for now he has found a way to make a singular promise.

Prada has created a unique retail space in New York. It is unlike any other store and provides the kind of experience that high-end fashion shoppers demand. The investment and effort it has made make the shopping experience impossible to copy and this allows many of the Prada goods sold to carry little or no evidence of a logo or trademark.

Reports of the death of logos are premature but it is clear that brands are no longer reliant upon them. Brands can now keep their promises through smart design and by providing a unique experience. This is a growing trend. Gucci and Prada confirm that brands are promises and a part of the promise is that they are exclusive or distinct. If counterfeiters can copy a logo then the brand promise is broken. Counterfeiters have done something good, however, in showing brands that simply slapping a logo on any old product is no longer good enough. The product or experience itself must promise something, not just the name.

Tim Greenhill makes the point that the primary purpose of brands is to be distinct: 'Brands are just about the only way that companies can differentiate their goods and services. Manufacturing and technology are so good these days that pretty much anything can be copied almost as soon as it is launched.'[3]

Where Mason and Greenhill's definitions converge is in their contention that brands are primarily emotional entities – promises and beliefs. This is a far cry from the AMA or Interbrand who contended in the past that brands were trademarks or products but is entirely in keeping with the latest actions of high fashion. Robbie Laughton, executive creative director of Wolff Olins at the time of writing, asserts, as does this book that 'the essence of any brand is a belief'.[4] It would be possible to leave our definition there but it is useful if we expand upon this and examine what in particular makes a belief into a brand.

CHAPTER 11

Turning beliefs into brands

Belief: Opinion, view, viewpoint, point of view, attitude, stance, stand, standpoint, position, perspective, contention, conviction, judgement, thinking, way of thinking, thought, idea, theory, hypothesis, thesis, interpretation, assumption, presumption, supposition, surmise, postulation, conclusion, deduction, inference, notion, impression, sense, feeling, fancy, hunch, faith, ideology.[1]

There are plenty of ways to describe a belief but they do not necessarily add clarity. What is the nature of belief? First, belief is an emotional entity, it has no physical form and it cannot be weighed or measured in any conventional sense. This gives the accountants a few problems when it comes to valuing a brand, something borne out by the experience of the Dotcom bubble. Belief, like all emotions, can be light or dark – positive or negative. What a brand strives for is to have people believe that it is good or beneficial. If a brand's audiences ever start to believe that the brand is malevolent then its days are likely to be numbered.

There is another important characteristic of belief and that is that it needs a vessel. In order to believe, we need something in which to believe. Brands have become receptacles for belief in today's society. Tim Greenhill contends that belief in brands has actually replaced belief in other entities such as the church or the police force. This also gives us a clue as to why brands exist in the first place and why, broadly speaking, people like them.

My granny says that when she first became aware of branded goods in the late 1920s, the reason she and her mother bought them was because they promised to be of a better quality than the unbranded goods. There was also the added benefit of knowing exactly where they were made and where the money would go. The promise of quality was a mainly functional benefit, the knowledge of origin, a predominantly emotional benefit.

Origin – known

A part of the appeal of a brand, particularly in fast-moving consumer goods (FMCGs) such as food and drink, is knowledge of its place of origin. We are what we eat and if we want to take care of ourselves we need to pay attention to what it is and where it comes from. This is a natural instinct and one that is codified in the ancient dietary laws of Judaism and Islam.

For many years, the laws of Kashrut and Halal could have been dismissed as archaic. They specify that animals should be fed non-meat products, should be slaughtered in a humane way and should be cleaned and cooked thoroughly. It is also possible to trace Kosher and Halal meat back to its place of origin. These kinds of laws were unfashionable, but if we consider the Bovine Spongiform Encephalopathy (BSE) crisis in the UK in the 1990s (BSE was also known as mad cow disease), we can see that the ancient laws could have prevented it happening.

Of course there are other, non-health-related reasons for wanting to know the place of origin of food. Traditionally, certain parts of the world have had exclusive access to ingredients and processes that created specific flavours. Indeed, many of the most recognizable names in food and drink are place names. Cheddar cheese from the little town near Bath is a fine product from England. Champagne, from the Champagne region of northern France is even more famous and Parmesan cheese from Parma has recently been a test case in the European courts for exactly what these kinds of names really mean.

Parmesan cheese has become particularly popular as an accompaniment to pasta dishes all over the world. As a result, commercial cheese-makers all over the world have come up with their own versions of it and called them Parmesan. The understanding was that Parmesan had become a generic for a certain type of hard cheese but European law decreed otherwise. Now, only hard cheese from Parma can be called Parmesan.

Similar cases could now be brought to protect the Cornish pasty, Eccles cake or maybe even the Swiss roll. Of course, manufacturers outside of these areas could still make these things but would have to call them something different. Thus, place names are proven to be protectable trademarks even though they may actually represent many different manufacturers from the same area.

If conveying a place of origin is important to a brand then there are other ways to do this than by name alone. Many brands through the years have used sonic branding for this goal, even to the point of being more than a little dishonest. Wall's used to make the most famous ice cream in the UK. As far back as the 1920s, they manufactured the bulk of the mainly vanilla ice cream consumed by the good people of Britain. Ice cream started its development in China around 1,000 years ago and came to mainland Europe, via Italy, as an exclusive delicacy in the late 1600s. It gradually moved from the table of royals to the upper classes and then finally into the diets of the common man, thanks, in the UK, to the Wall family.

By the 1970s, ice cream was ubiquitous and even a little boring so Wall's tried to innovate. They made ice cream in all shapes and flavours but the brand they launched in 1980, the Cornetto, has proved to be the most enduring. The product itself is an ice cream-filled cone, sprayed on the inside with chocolate to keep it crispy. It is a tasty ice cream but its success is put down as much to the classic sonic branding as it is to the innovative manufacturing techniques.

In order to differentiate the Cornetto from its more prosaic, British ice creams, Wall's decided to position the brand as quintessentially Italian, that nation being famous for its ice creams. To do this, they used the name and Italian images in the advertising but it was the sonic branding that resonated with consumers to such an extent that one of the most famous Italian traditional songs is still, 23 years later, a brand property of Cornetto. 'O Sole Mio' (also the tune to Elvis' hit 'It's Now or Never') was given new lyrics and within just a few months of the TV commercials airing, 'Just One Cornetto' became the most famous Italian song in the UK. In the list of the *100 Greatest TV Ads*,[2] compiled by Channel 4 and *The Times* in 2000, the campaign was voted in at number 23, despite being off-air for more than 15 years.

Cornetto was made in Britain, by a British firm but as far as the eating public were concerned it was as Italian as spaghetti hoops. It was so successful that Wall's followed it up with the Italian-sounding Viennetta and an entire sub-brand called Gino Ginelli, which had its own, less resonant sonic branding.

As if that were not enough faux-Italian products from Unilever (Wall's parent company) the Cornetto lessons were carried through to the launch of Ragu pasta sauces in the UK, whose Italian operatic sonics claimed: 'Ragu, Ragu, Ragu, Ragu. Brings the Italian out in you! Made in the UK.'

Both functional and emotional benefits meant that the brand was something to be trusted and something in which to believe. Beyond these immediate benefits, brands became a matter of self-expression and pride for the makers and customers. Brands still provide functional and emotional benefits. We have to believe that we will gain at least one of them if we are to believe in a specific brand.

As already stated, belief is a strange concept that is not easily described but I like to think of belief as being an 'investment of emotions' and where the emotional investment is considered to have a beneficial end state, as with brands, then it can be said to be 'positive'. Treating belief as an investment allows us to see how important belief is to a brand. We know that without investment, all entities fail.

Positive emotional investment (PEI), a catch-all term for such concepts as love, caring and nurturing, is what leads people into making all the other investments that brands require: time, capital or purchase. Quite simply, the more people that invest, the stronger a brand becomes. That PEI is actually at the top of the investment hierarchy, far beyond the kind of financial investments usually talked about, can be demonstrated through a simple case study of how a belief is at the origin of a brand.

Figure 11.1 Belief

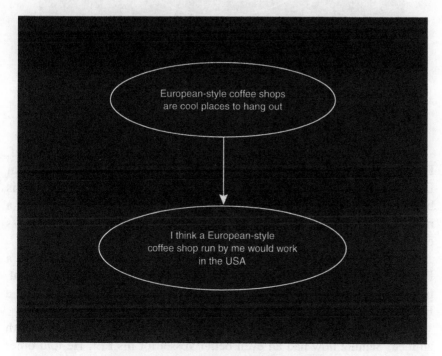

Figure 11.2 Belief becomes an idea

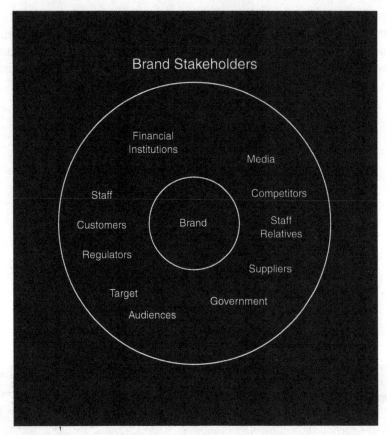

Figure 11.3 Brand stakeholders

All brands start with a person or small group of people who share a belief. For example, Starbucks was apparently founded on the belief that European-style coffee shops were cool places to hang out. Let us put this belief in a little box so we can examine it. It gives us a starting point for a neat chart that we can use to define the essence of a brand and the process of branding.

Howard Schultz, the founder of Starbucks as we know it, then made a PEI and started telling people how good these places were. More than that, he invested his time into coming up with an idea. His idea was to open a European-style coffee shop in the United States.

At this point, the idea became more important than the initial belief. With an idea, Schultz now had an even better vessel for his PEI. He told other people his idea and because of his enthusiasm, they agreed with him.

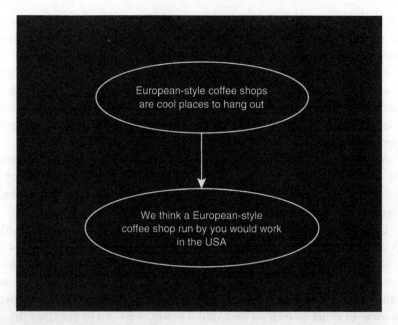

Figure 11.4 Stakeholders' share in the belief and idea – Starbucks

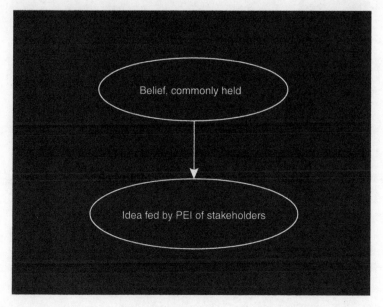

Figure 11.5 Stakeholders' share in the belief and idea – abstract

The more people he told, the more he was told in return that his was a good idea. In this way, he encouraged other people to make a PEI into his idea. Each person that was convinced became a stakeholder in the brand.

The stakeholder is a key component of a modern brand definition. Stakeholders are all the people who believe in a brand, from the founder's mother to the customer in a remote country. It is the broadest definition of a brand's constituency and acknowledges that family, staff, the financial world, the media and every customer are important to the brand.

As the number of stakeholders grew from one, Howard Schultz, to many, the 'I' of idea became a 'we'. A momentum built and has been building ever since on a big wave of PEI. This is shown in particular and abstract in Figures 11.4 and 11.5.

This is a simple model but it is not yet a brand because it is still only an idea, albeit a popular one. Ideas exist on an ethereal plain and it would be very hard for even a talented businessman like Howard Schultz to generate wealth, financial or emotional, simply from an idea. It is always worth remembering that ideas are not ownable in law. It is impossible to copyright an idea. In order to turn an idea into a brand, we need to consider the challenge of making something tangible, something real-worldly, so that many more people can believe in it.

CHAPTER 12

Generating belief — the greatest story ever told

If we accept that brands are centred on beliefs then it makes sense to define branding as the generation of belief: a process whereby we ask stakeholders to make a positive emotional investment (PEI) into a brand. In trying to discover how to convince people to believe, we find that our subject crosses the paths of religion, philosophy and psychology. The former, because no other movement in human history has generated more belief than the evangelizing religion of Christianity and the two 'P's because the great thinkers of the world have spent a lot of time over the centuries working out the nature of belief.

The Church of England today is well aware that it is a brand. It is easy to see that it is an organization founded upon belief but we must also recognize that it exists physically, as do all other branches of the Christian church. If we go back 2,000 years to the foundations of Christianity and examine the challenge that was faced by the early Christians, we can see that the process of evangelizing, of converting non-believers to believers, can be examined for the purpose of defining a brand. It involved the same issue that was faced by Schultz or the McDonald's: making tangible the intangible – turning ethereal ideas into things that exist in the real world.

It is worth stating, however, that whereas today's branding industry is based upon conscious emotional engineering, the religious movement we are referencing was instinctive, intuitive and motivated by a desire for a 'better' world. The central belief of the first Christians was that Jesus was the Messiah; indeed this still forms the crux of Christianity today, some 2,000 years later. The ideas that stemmed from this were many and varied but the most important idea the early followers had was that the world would be a better place if other people shared their belief in Jesus and the Gospel.

Spiritually, to follow a religious path is deep and complex and we will not go into any religion's relative merits here. But on a purely practical level, how did the early Christians go about convincing people to believe? First, the early Christians had a natural desire to differentiate themselves from those who held alternate beliefs and had different values. Differentiation was very important. How otherwise would any new Christians know what they were becoming? The most important lesson in differentiation that Christianity gives us is that it was founded upon a set of values. These values are, essentially, what convinced the first people to convert to Christianity and what gave early Christians their main identity. It is also possible to assert that the values would have been at the centre of everything done by the early Christians.

Jumping forward to 1972, Milton Rokeach provides the best definition of a value I have ever read in his book *The Nature of Human Values*: 'An enduring belief that a specific mode of conduct or end state of existence is personally or socially preferable to an opposite or converse mode of conduct or end state of existence.'[1] For simplicity's sake, we will assert that the value set of the early Christians was the Ten Commandments. The Ten Commandments are the basis for the moral law of most of the world's people, so it is fair to make this simplification though, of course, there are now many more complex values that have been added over the centuries.

To differentiate is to have an identity that is distinct from everything else. The Christian identity was created primarily through living according to the values of Christianity and secondarily through naming the religion and identifying it with symbols. The name was obviously chosen as descriptive, Christ having a literal translation as 'anointed' or 'messiah'. The fish symbol, representing Jesus the fisherman, is said to have been developed by those Christians who lived under repression and used it to identify their beliefs without alerting those who would harm them. Subsequently, however, it was adopted as universal symbol for Christianity, as was the crucifix, one of the most powerful symbols in the world today. There are other symbols too, such as the ox, lion, man and eagle that represent the four evangelists.

In the 2,000 years since it all began, Christianity has fragmented but the central belief, the value set, the name and the symbols have remained largely unaltered. It is the consistency with which these identifying elements have been applied all over the world that has given Christianity its strength and created the brand of the religion. The model as it relates to that of a brand can be viewed in Figures 12.1 and 12.2.

Christianity, of course, has developed over the last 1,700 years since the Gospel was written and in that time, it has had the opportunity to explore many other, sophisticated ways in which to create belief by representing its ideas in the physical realm. These have become a part of experience of

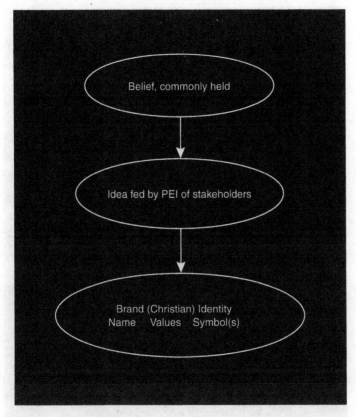

Figure 12.1   Christianity as a brand

being a Christian. Layered on top of the values, name and symbols have been many additional, powerful communicators. Again, these secondary elements have been created on human instinct for the greater good, rather than as emotional engineering but they have provided the branding industry with a blueprint.

Without going into too much detail, it is easy to identify how the churches of Europe developed an architectural style that strongly differentiates church buildings from commercial or residential ones, or those belonging to other religions. Further to that, one can identify how ranges of apparel have been developed over the centuries and how language has been used to identify one church from another. Additionally, festivals, icons and foods, among many other things, have been incorporated into the identities of all branches of Christianity.

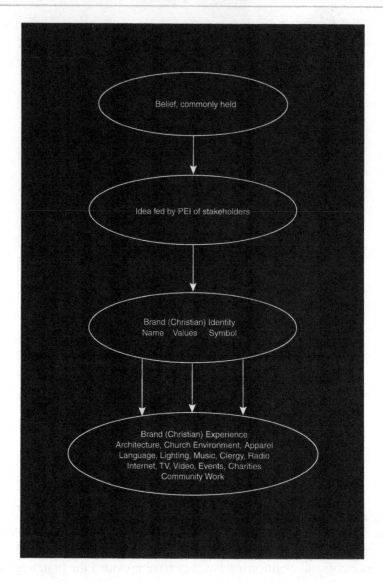

Figure 12.2 Christianity as a brand and experience

Some denominations, such as the Church of England, now use the Internet as a means of disseminating information and print media have been used for centuries already. Television programming is also important for any Christian churches, particularly in the United States where the televangelist is a major cultural phenomenon.

It is easy, if a little uncomfortable, to see the parallels with brands such as McDonald's who have developed along very similar lines through architecture, uniforms, iconography, event days and the use of every medium available. The problem is that the goals of businesses in capitalist democracies have tended to revolve around the creation of profit rather than the spread of moral and ethical allegories. Nonetheless, businesses have been able to harness the same communications power as organized religions in order to have stakeholders believe in their brands and supply profit as a result of faith.

Only history and experience give a perspective on this. Indeed, it may only be in 2003 that we truly understand how badly some businesses have betrayed the faith of their stakeholders. The Enron and WorldCom stories make ugly reading, showing us that brands are sometimes used as smokescreens while the unscrupulous profit from stakeholder's misplaced faith.

Some religious music history

Perhaps the most powerful identifier that has been adopted by almost all parts of the Christian church, and indeed by many other religions, is of particular relevance to this book – music. It has also, as we will see in later chapters, been used by many famous brands. All cultures are thought to have been musical since the dawn of man, but the Christian church first adopted music, in a formal sense, around AD 600. Pope Gregory I created a system to explain the musical scales that the church had employed, uncodified, up until that time. Thanks to Pope Gregory, we have the names of the scales: A, B, C and so on that are still employed today.

Gregory's name gave us the Gregorian chant, the form and singing of which also survives today and was the basis for a world-wide hit album in the 1990s. In fact, the monks that began chanting their prayers helped create the basis for modern music, with Guido of Arezzo taking particular credit for the invention of modern musical notation.

From the Middle Ages up until the Renaissance, the development of what is known as western music was largely in the hands of the Catholic church, with most of the great works of the time devised to accompany the Latin mass. Sung mass was mirrored by the development of hymns, which were mainly psalms set to music. The sheer joy of the music, coupled with the phenomena of memorability, whereby words sung became fixed in the head, made music enduringly popular in Christianity.

Vivaldi was an employee of the Catholic church; most of Handel's work was written to lyrics from the Bible; and Bach was cantor of the church of St Thomas in

Leipzig. In fact, the instrument that made Bach famous, the organ, was routinely installed in churches and is still associated with Christian music today. Other examples of the huge canon of religious music include the 'Wedding March', written by Felix Mendelssohn in the early nineteenth century and the various funeral marches, of which Fredrick Chopin's 'Sonata Opus 35 for Piano' is probably the most famous – a range of music truly reflecting the whole spectrum of human emotions.

Music has, therefore, been central to Christianity for at least 1,400 years and almost certainly longer. Even for modern music genres, many of the most influential artists have taken cues from Christian music. Elvis's main influence was gospel as it was for Destiny's Child and innumerable rhythm and blues artists.

As already mentioned, music has also played a part in the other great religions of the world. Singing is an ancient activity, though we know little of it because we had no way of recording it until Thomas Edison invented the phonograph on 12 August 1877. Even then, the quality of the recording was so poor that he lost interest after making only a few recordings. If recording devices had been around for many thousands of years we might have a very different perspective on how even ancient man may have used music as a communicator.

The Islamic call to prayer is as close to the ancient traditions of singing as can be traced in the modern world and Islam has always used music and chanting as an aid to prayer. For accuracy, however, one must note that the call to prayer and chanting of the Qur'an are not considered music or singing within the faith. *Musiqa* in Arabic refers to instrumental, popular music which in some interpretations of the Qur'an is not to be encouraged. Local cultures within the Islamic world however, have musical traditions that predate the spread of Islam and may actually be at odds with the largely non-musical teachings of the religion.

Eastern religions too have used music as an aid to prayer or meditation. The Tibetan chanting bowls, used within Buddhist meditation, are an example. Unlike Islam, Buddhism embraces all forms of music, having three broad categories: folk music, art music and sacred chanting or instrumental music. Buddhist chant was descended from an Indian tradition around 400 BC. It is known that professional Buddhist chanters were plying their trade in Korea by about the eighth century when a Silla monk named Chin'gam travelled to T'ang, China, learned to chant and then returned to teach many pupils. Buddhist folk and art music, of course, are products of the local cultures of Asia. China in particular has a very long musical tradition, stretching back some 3,000 years, the spread of which was advocated by Confucius.

Judaism is a very musical religion with two distinct traditions. Ashkenazi music tends towards minor keys and haunting melodies, while the more musically pleasing Sephardic tradition employs more major keys and joyful melodies. There is also a musical instrument, the shofar, which plays a central role for all Jews on their holiest days; the New Year and Day of Atonement. This instrument, fashioned from a ram's horn, echoes back many thousands of years and is referenced in the Bible many times, particularly in relation to the battle of Jericho.

Today, hearing a Buddhist chant or the sound of the shofar is a haunting experience. There is something in their resonance that feels ancient and connected with the Earth. Their power, like that of all music, is in tapping into our collective unconscious and creating powerful emotional responses. This is why music has been used by people through the ages to help create belief. Music heightens our emotional state and makes us more open to ideas and suggestions.

CHAPTER 13

Any belief can become a brand

We have taken some wide-ranging views of brands, from people, to religions, through to McDonald's. What we have shown is that anything that starts with a belief can become a brand. Well, actually we have not shown that at all. We have asserted brands require a positive emotional investment (PEI) and this needs a little more explanation because it is the 'positive' that determines which beliefs can become brands.

Any idea or belief held by any one person can, given the right circumstances, be believed in by another. This being the case, no matter how wild or deviant an idea, it is possible, in theory, that it can become a brand. It is not possible in practice, however, and this has much to do with the nature of human belief and the concept of sustainability.

We have shown that consistency is an important factor. The belief, idea and values must be consistently held and human history shows us that positive beliefs and ideas have a much better chance of being held in the long run than negative beliefs. It is the long run that is of interest to brands because they only exist for as long as they are believed in – for as long as they are in receipt of PEI.

If you have ever seen *Star Wars*, you will know that good will always triumph over evil. This is not just fantasy. *Star Wars* resonates with so many people because we want to believe that in our world, optimism and positivity are more powerful emotional forces than negativity and pessimism. The Rebel Alliance versus the Empire is an ancient story repackaged. It is rational and entirely Darwinian to conclude that positive, creative, beneficial forces in this world will ultimately triumph over the negative, destructive forces. This is human nature; it is the stuff of every myth and legend. This belief is woven deep into the fabric of society and long may it be so.

What it means for brands is that any negative brand cannot survive for long because ultimately people want benefits and benefits are, by definition, positive. There have been very few 'dark' brands. One example was Death cigarettes, launched in the United Kingdom in the 1980s as the first tobacco brand that actually acknowledged it was going to kill you. They are no longer on sale because there were no long-term benefits associated with them. Functionally they were the same as other brands and emotionally, after the morbid joke had worn of, they made disturbing self-expression. Thus, Death cigarettes are not a brand any more, merely a piece of social history.

It is only in the last ten years that the concept of sustainability has crept into brand thinking but it is now recognized as being absolutely essential for the future success of brands. The lesson that sustainability over time is worthy of close attention has only become apparent in hindsight.

It took the Dot.Com bubble to burst to teach a new generation that, apparently, great brands can die, quickly and seemingly without warning. Now that we have seen generations of brands come and go, we can really start to understand what makes a brand and what makes a flash in the pan. The concept of sustainability recognizes that time is a factor in business. This may be obvious to some, but business history is littered with short-sighted strategies that seemed perfectly sound for the five minutes after they were conceived.

Some examples of brands that failed to recognize the critical nature of sustainability? How about Boo.com or Enron? Going back a little further, maybe Laker or DeLorean? In the dim past you might point to brands such as Rolls Razor or Austin Morris. The reasons why all these brands died are varied but the fact is they are dead. That means they were not sustainable; that means they are not brands any more.

Boo.com was meant to change the way the world shopped. Fronted by a virtual personality and offering the most comprehensive way to view and select items to buy were great ideas and undoubtedly, they will one day be successful – but not for Boo.com. Technology could not keep up with the ideas and 56k modems cannot handle animated personal web-shoppers. Boo.com did things that were criminally stupid in the name of its brand and really took brand thinking to one of its low-points. It spent many fortunes on advertising and public relations. It also spent a fortune on first-class travel, fresh cut flowers and fancy offices. It ignored the real business of retail and decided to push on with its own methods and systems – methods and systems that did not work and did not even generate enough revenue to pay for the fresh flowers every morning. The business spent far too much money in the name of their brand, acting out the worst cliché of a lottery winner. The opportunity was wasted and Boo's shareholders paid the price for trusting in an unproven revenue model. The frustration of this story is that those who believed in the brand saw some great social benefits to its growth and success. They genuinely believed in a better world with new ways to shop and quicker routes to market.

Freddie Laker also had good ideas and a good business. That was, until he took on British Airways (BA) in a price war. He was right – people were being over-charged – but the price war he started was unsustainable. Simply, he had not thought through his strategy and come to the obvious conclusion that he could not keep it going for long enough to defeat BA who had the might of the British government backing them up.

What Boo and Laker and countless other brand failures teach us is that the generation of financial wealth must be at the heart of a commercial brand and everything it does. No matter how good the idea or how strong the belief, if it cannot make money it will not be a successful brand.

It is lucky that we can learn from history but I must share a little concern I have about all the brand experts to whom Paul and I spoke in researching this book. Not one of them mentioned financial viability as being central to brands and almost all of them were working predominately in the commercial world.

Hubris is a major factor in many brand failures. Sometimes pride is justified but when it is overweening in relation to business activities, there is bound to be a fall. When those who work for a brand are guilty of lies and hubris, they are failing to make a PEI in the brand. If this happens, then why should other stakeholders continue their PEI in the brand?

Corporate social responsibility (CSR) has grown as a business discipline to serve the emotional sustainability of brands. In effect, it is a modern reworking of ethics and morals. It adds these factors to the value set of commercial brands where previously they have been present primarily in social brands such as religions. As far as CSR goes, it is very welcome, but it is widely thought that most businesses are currently only paying lip-service to the concept and that a seismic change is required in the way business is conducted in the capitalist democracy in order to generate true sustainability.

We have lauded McDonald's as being one of the brands that taught the world what a brand is but there are worrying signs that McDonald's may not be a sustainable brand into the twenty-first century. Its social responsibility has been called severely into question and though it has survived the onslaught so far, it could tumble at any time. Right now, a class action in the United States is being brought against McDonald's with the accusation that the company has caused many of its most loyal stakeholders to become obese. It is a very interesting case, with echoes of similar actions brought against the tobacco industry in the 1990s.

The quote from *Fast Food Nation* (in Chapter 9) showed use that the aim of the McDonald's communication was to 'make the customers believe that McDonald's is their "Trusted Friend"'. It may be semantics but this is different to actually *being* a trusted friend. If McDonald's stakeholders come to believe that they have been manipulated and that McDonald's was never really on their side, then it is entirely possible that the whole brand could become worthless almost overnight.

This is unlikely, because those of us who consume a moderate quantity of burgers and who understand the possible dietary implications will probably stick with the brand for a while. What further damage, though, could be done to the brand by the sight of branches closing down? Or of staff being laid off and revealing dark secrets? It would not take long once the PEI was gone. It is easy to see how the brand could die as a result of stakeholders learning to believe it had malevolent values or methods. Stakeholders could simply walk away and never go back. There is an alternative future for McDonald's, however, and it is one that could happen even if they lose their US court case.

If the stakeholders, rather than walk away, decide that they believe in Speedee Service and find the Big Mac so tasty they could not live without it, they can effect change. Stakeholders have the power to change the way companies operate and they will do this if they care enough or if they have made such a large PEI that they feel they cannot walk away without trying to help. Stakeholders can help in many ways. Staff and customers alike might lobby company executives with suggestions for a better way. This kind of action by stakeholders, where the people who believe in a brand seek to change the way it behaves in the name of long-term sustainability, is perhaps the most important and historically undervalued asset of any brand. For proof, look no further than the campaign for 'real Coke' to see how a brand that listens can prosper even in adversity.

Companies like ESSO and McDonald's should actually count themselves lucky that there are people out there who care enough to let them know their dissatisfaction, because the feedback of these stakeholders is what might really create brand sustainability – if the brands listen and learn.

The brand is a system, created and fed by the PEI of stakeholders at every level from the first believer to the final customer. Its output is made up of functional or emotional benefits.

As such, brands are rather like any of the creations of man. As Shoeless Jackson said in *Field of Dreams* 'if you build it, they will come'. Essentially, if we put the effort in to create a brand then somewhere down the line someone is going to enjoy a benefit. There is a parallel with art in this sense and in many others. The great brands were not created out of conscious science or numbers but out of the human instinct to interpret beliefs and ideas in artistic ways. This has been recognized by academia.

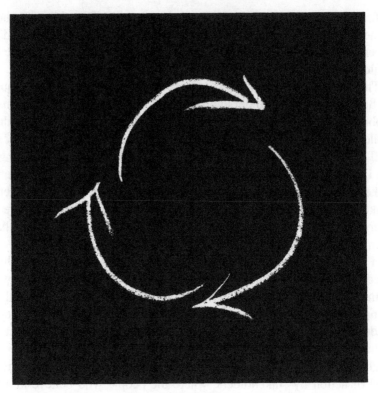

Figure 13.1   Sustainability requires a feedback system

Schmitt and Simonson, entitled their incredibly quotable 1997 book about brands, *Marketing Aesthetics*. In it, they herald a new paradigm in marketing, stating that the future of brands is defined by the appeal of their aesthetics.[1] What they were actually heralding was the work of artists like Eastman and the McDonald brothers. These people had no Interbrand to advise them and yet they were able to create great brands because they were creative people – Eastman a photographer and the McDonald's movie set makers. The contributions to our culture made by these guys were vast and in many ways just as important artistically as any Van Gogh.

The art is still being practised by those entrepreneurial enough to seek to establish new brands. Robbie Laughton of Wolf Olins and Paul Fulberg, editor of this book, cite Innocent, the makers of juice drinks as being an outstanding new brand. It was created and is still being developed in-house, by the founders of the business. Similarly, I think that Lush, an organic toiletries and cosmetics company, is one of the best new brands today. Though it is now a multinational organization, it is still headquartered above the original shop in Poole in Dorset, where all aspects of the brand can still be developed with the original belief in view.

Innocent and Lush are the true flag-carriers for branding, because they are showing that they have the belief and the ideas to make the brand come to life. They have identified the brand well and as they develop they will work on all aspects of the experience to ensure that it is consistent with their beliefs. They are really carrying out branding because they view the brand as a whole in everything they do. They are managing their brands consistently with long-term success as the goal. The founders have the brand at heart and understand its every nuance. The challenge for them now is to try to express the nuances of their brand in such as way as the next or expanded generations can continue their work and up the PEI.

The visionary founders of brands, eventually, have to hire other people to carry on for them or to fill in the gaps in their knowledge. So, employees or agencies are hired. The important thing is that these new people have to be convinced of the central belief and ideas before they can help identify or create the experience of the brand. In recent years, the education of staff and agencies has become a key part of the branding industry offering. It is probably, in the long run, the most important task of all; generating belief among staff so that they can go out and generate belief among other stakeholders. Internal branding goes straight to the heart of what we have shown a brand is all about and is an essential task of the brand guardian, ensuring that those who manage the many facets of a brand do the right thing. Music has a role to play but unfortunately, that is a subject for another book.

CHAPTER 14

Definition of a brand

An idea, stemming from belief, that through its consistent identity, experience and the positive emotional investment (PEI) of stakeholders, creates sustainable benefits.

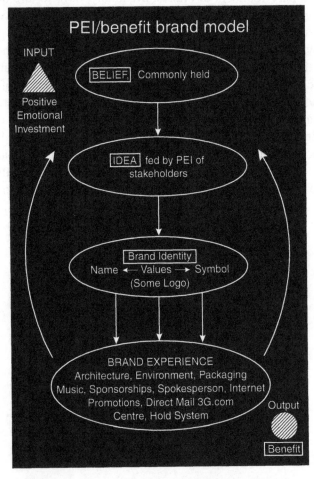

Figure 14.1 The PEI/benefit brand model

CHAPTER 15

Branding

If individuals are best at brand creation, it is fair to say that other activities concerned with expressing the brand will usually be better handled by those with expertise in their own field such as designers or advertising agencies. These partners to the creators of the brand are involved in 'branding', which is a special term all on its own and needs its own definition. We could assert that branding is just everything to do with a brand but that would be overly simplistic. Branding is primarily concerned with consistency between the ideas of a brand and the way it expresses itself in terms of its identity and the experience it offers. It is important we remember this because in the drive for creativity and the new, new thing, consistency is usually the first casualty.

Some brands, however, have managed to be interesting and engaging while maintaining very high levels of consistency over many, many years. The world's top ten brands, as shown in Figure 15.1, are models of consistency. They are all brands that evolve their brand expressions slowly and with an eye to the past as well as the future.

If we examine a few of them, we can begin to describe the characteristics of these brands and learn some lessons about what is likely to constitute successful branding. In contrast to the previous section on brands, we will start with our definition of branding as a point of reference. Successful branding is the creation and consistent management of distinct, memorable, flexible and honest brand identity and experience.

Distinct

Coca-Cola was invented in 1886 by a pharmacist, John Pemberton, of Atlanta, Georgia. He sold his syrup, mixed with carbonated water, at the nearby Jacob's Pharmacy. Together with his book-keeper he named the product, and it is his book-keeper's writing that can still be viewed in the trademark name of the company. This trademark was seen very early on

BRAND 2001	BRAND VALUE $m
1. Coca-Cola	68,945
2. Microsoft	65,068
3. IBM	52,752
4. GE	42,396
5. Nokia	35,035
6. Intel	34,665
7. Disney	32,591
8. Ford	30,092
9. McDonald's	25,289
10. AT&T	22,828

in the history of the company as being important and it has been protected by law since the product was launched.

The drink that Pemberton invented was distinct from anything else available at the time. In colour and taste it was new and utterly different and this, together with the business acumen of Asa Candler, who bought the Coca-Cola Company from its founder, is what helped it make its impact upon the world.

Earlier in this section, we showed that differentiation was fundamental to brand-owners from the Syrian sandal maker to the early Christians and the McDonald brothers. To be distinct is to be different from everyone and everything else and this is absolutely of the essence of a brand's identity. It is relatively easy to be distinct when an identity or product is new, as Coca-Cola was in 1886, but to maintain distinctiveness over time takes a lot of hard work. For a start, we are all plagiarists and every new idea will spawn a million copies as soon as it is out there.

It took only 12 years for Caleb Bradham of North Carolina to come up with a recipe for a cola nut drink. Although originally called 'Brad's Drink', it was soon renamed as Pepsi-Cola and became a serious competitor to Coca-Cola.

The recipes for the products were the original reasons for their popularity and continue to be so. It is worth remembering that the major failures in the histories of both brands have been associated with the recipes. Pepsi was declared bankrupt for the second time in 1931. In the same year, the formula was changed and the company has gone from strength to strength since. Similarly, when Coca-Cola made a drastic change to its formula in 1985, it lost its position as number one almost overnight. Only on the reintroduction of 'Classic' Coke did it start to revive its fortunes. The impact of these two events clearly shows that the distinctive nature of the product itself is the most important factor in consumer purchasing of the brands. How, though, have they managed to remain distinct from one another when most people cannot tell them apart in blind tasting?

The two rivals have given the world one of its best case studies in how to maintain the distinctiveness of brands when the commodity itself is so obviously similar and the simplified lesson from this battle is that every possible touchpoint should be consistent with the brand message and intellectual property must be fiercely protected. When Coca-Cola first became interested in protecting its position against its rival, around 1916, it commissioned the Root Glass Company of Terre Haute, Indiana, to create a distinctive bottle. The contour shape, with its exciting, feminine curves, remains a signature of the brand that has never been successfully copied, though Virgin Cola tried to with its 'Pammie' bottle, nicknamed for Pamela

Andersen, the *Baywatch* actress whose curves are said to have been an inspiration.

Coca-Cola's position as the world's number one brand owes much to Robert Woodruff, the third visionary in its history. From 1919 until 1960, he oversaw the expansion of the brand throughout the world. This was done through distinctive point-of-sale design, sponsorships and advertising. He introduced six-packs, liveried cool-boxes and liveried bottle openers, fitted in houses free by door-to-door female representatives. He also sponsored the 1928 US team for the Olympics in Amsterdam, dog-sled races in Canada and bullfights in Spain. 'Think global, act local' was truly a tenet of Coke's global drive for distinctiveness.

The war was also viewed, rather disturbingly, as a great opportunity for Coke's expansion. Woodruff famously decreed that every US soldier, wherever in the world, should have access to a five cent bottle of Coke. This was most definitely a loss-leader but the legacy of brand association between a liberating army and a soft drink is fascinating and astounding. The post-war expansion of the US economy allowed many years of unbroken growth for Coke too but while it had focused upon product, packaging and delivering the drinking experience to gain its place in the hearts of its stakeholders, Pepsi had been following a different strategy, focusing upon advertising and entertainment.

Pepsi had always been a company that advertised; its first press ad was in 1902 but it was not until Walter S. Mack Jr was elected president of the Pepsi-Cola Company in 1938 that Pepsi became a business led by its marketing strategy. From the first US national radio jingle in 1940 to the 'turn the world blue' activity of the 1990s, Pepsi has sought out every advertising and public relations opportunity to differentiate itself from the competition. In many ways, it has had to work harder than Coca-Cola, whose classic status requires it only to carry on doing what it has always done to succeed. Pepsi, meanwhile has had to put the first can in space (on the shuttle in 1985) and constantly update its positioning from 'Exhilarating, Invigorating, Aids Digestion' in 1903 to 'The Joy of Pepsi' in 2002.

Music has been at the heart of the Pepsi strategy since 1940, with everyone from Ray Charles through Michael Jackson to Britney Spears representing the brand. Pepsi has even been sponsoring charts in the UK for some 20 years. Even so, Pepsi has been overshadowed in sonic branding terms by Coke, who were really copying Pepsi when they released 'I'd Like to Buy the World a Coke' in 1971. In doing so, however they created the biggest brand-music hit of all time. A theory as to why this stands out despite Pepsi's 60-year association with popular music is that Pepsi has always sponsored the music of others. In many ways, Pepsi helped make Madonna famous, as they did Boyzone and Hear'say in the UK (thanks Pepsi). Coke, however, made itself famous through its creation of music rather than endorsement of it.

Clearly, the sonic strategies of the two companies are important and perhaps put into sharp relief the overriding benefits of creating one's own, distinct sonic branding rather than borrowing the latest musical fashion every year. Coca-Cola is the classic brand, the number one brand in the world and its brand communications use commissioned music that makes the brand distinct and makes the brand the star.

Every brand faces the challenge of maintaining its distinctiveness. McDonald's has been openly copied ever since it first opened for business. Seattle's Best, Tulley's and Coffee Republic jumped on the Starbucks bandwagon almost before it turned a wheel. The successful brands, like Coca-Cola, are the ones that find out what it is that makes them distinct in the minds of stakeholders and protect that uniqueness with innovation, the trademark system engaging creativity at every brand touchpoint from advertising to the bottle.

Memorable

Remembering is an intrinsic part of human nature. In the theogony of the ancient Greeks, the nine muses, of epic poetry, history, tragedy and so on, were the daughters of the goddess Mnemosyne (Greek for memory) by their father Zeus, King of the Gods. Memory allows us to learn and to know so it is clearly advantageous for brands to be extremely memorable. For a long time, people involved in branding have recognized that being memorable is one of the most important goals of any brand or brand communication. It is the common understanding that there has to be something in a brand that means that the next time it is encountered through any touchpoint, it will be remembered.

The classic measures of the effectiveness of advertising have sought to quantify memorability together with awareness and persuasion. In the context of advertising, memorability refers to the level to which an audience, after exposure to an ad, is able to retain the information presented. Memorability in advertising is viewed as most important for new brands but it is clear that there is little point to any brand communication if it is to go in one ear and straight out the other.

Rather than relying upon ads to be memorable, ideally, memorability will flow directly from that which makes the brand distinct. In the case of

Disney, the seventh most valuable brand in the world according to Interbrand, this is most definitely the case. The Disney offering is an extremely rich experience ranging from children's cuddly toys to DVDs full of music and fantastic animated characters. As if they were not enough to be memorable, Disney has its theme parks which provide an immersive experience for every visitor. Disney's targeting people when they are young and impressionable gives it an immediate advantage in generating memorability. What could be more memorable than your favourite toy or film when you are a small child or your first holiday to Disneyland?

Even for those of us who grew up during the leanest of times for Disney's creativity, the 1970s, we were encouraged to watch reruns of the classic movies: *Dumbo*, *Snow White* and *Cinderella* on TV as well as clip shows from the Disney archive, presented by Rolf Harris as Christmas specials. I remember visiting *Snow White* world at a large department store in London when I was around four years old. The magic of the experience has stayed with me ever since and it is clear that Disney's products and brands are intrinsically memorable.

It is not a coincidence that Disney is probably the most musically active brand in the world. More like Coke than Pepsi, Disney has always created its own music and used it to further revenue generation and further the brand. For all the reasons discussed earlier, the use of music by Disney has greatly enhanced the memorability of its brand touchpoints. The greatest hits of Disney have been used consistently between the theme parks, movies, TV channels, DVDs, CDs, toys and stores. They have won Oscars and are sung by school choirs.

As timeless works, too, they will be handed from generation to generation. Currently, a dancing Tigger from *Winnie the Pooh* seems to be the favourite toy of many of my friends' children. I asked a few of the parents why they chose to buy Tigger? The universal answer was that they had a Tigger themselves when they were young and it was one of their favourite toys. This is a clear demonstration of how useful it can be to make an indelible mark upon the memory with your brand.

Not all brands are so lucky, though, as to offer their stakeholders the kind of rich, child-focused, memorable experience as Disney. Indeed, the core offering of some brands is so unmemorable as to almost not register at all. Intel makes the microchips that, unseen, power computers. When consumers have no physical or emotional connection with the products themselves, how should a brand generate memorability? The Intel strategy has been built around a single device, a sonic logo, whose main purpose is as a mnemonic or aid to memory. By paying for this mnemonic device to be included in the advertising of all the computers that contain Intel chips, the brand has achieved a status and a level of memorability that far outweighs the immediate impact of the product or brand on people's lives.

With memorability being so fundamental to branding, it is fairly simple to take any list of brands and identify what, why and how they have become primarily memorable. What will spring to my mind, however, will be very different to the next person. Every memory is different having been formed from a unique perspective. Of the top ten brands, perhaps only Intel is memorable for a reason that would instantly be agreed upon by all people. The others have much richer histories and communications strategies and will have created very different textures in our individual heads.

Flexible

Concepts such as brand stretch, how far a brand's influence spreads and brand extension, new products under an existing brand name, have become familiar to anyone working with brands. In many cases, the success that can be gained from stretching or extending brands will depend upon the inherent flexibility of the identity of the brand. The best identities work across many different platforms, countries and audiences. All of the top ten brands have global reach and their identifying name, values and symbols are flexible enough to mean something consistent to many different audiences.

The name is often the least flexible part of any brand identity, relying as it does on the written language. There are many famous examples of brand names that meant one perfectly good thing in one country but had totally different meanings in another. Brand names such as Grated Fanny (a Latin American tinned tuna) or Sor-bits (a Danish chewing gum), lack the flexibility to work in English-speaking countries. We can expect these brands never to make the global top ten, whose names are suitably neutral to function well all over the world. The literal translations of names make their selection inherently difficult and the need for consistent naming makes this the least flexible component of any identity. Of the top ten global brands, not one has changed its name in living memory. Just imagine how much communications budget would be required by Ford if it were to change its name.

To change the colour of an identity, as Pepsi did in the mid-1990s, is also a very big deal, requiring huge investments to let stakeholders know how and why the brand's colours have changed. For Pepsi, the need to differentiate itself from Coke was deemed a good enough reason to justify the investment. By contrast, sonic identities are incredibly flexible and the ability to change and adapt to suit their context is one of their great strengths. Similarly, changing the logo or symbol of a brand necessitates big budget commitments. Imagine if McDonald's changed its 'M' to a different symbol? It would have a huge impact upon the business.

The names, colours and symbols of brands need to be distinctive and consistent. As a result, they are very rarely played with. Colours stay the same, graphic ratios are specified and names are sacrosanct. Sonic elements of identity, however, can be designed for change and alteration as often as required. Unlike other elements of identity, the inherent nature of sound and music in particular makes adaptation a massive opportunity for brands that have invested in the right sonic identity.

Intel, the most noticeable of the sonic branders, has reworked its sonic logo at least four times since it was launched ten years ago. Most people are completely unaware, yet the logo has changed quite significantly, becoming richer in its musical complexity and at the same time using ultra-contemporary sounds to maintain its cutting edge technology feel. Crucially, the one thing that has not changed in the Intel sonic logo is the melody. With a consistent melody in place, sonic identities can be rearranged but still maintain their essence. As an example from the purely musical world, Frank Sinatra and the Sex Pistols both recorded the same song, 'My Way'. Their versions are utterly different and appeal to different audiences. Frank is all smooth crooning, Jon Lydon is angry punk, but despite the different attitude and 'colour' of the recordings, the melody at their heart is still the same and recognizable. This flexibility gives those working with sonic branding the opportunity to alter an identity without changing it. The emotions can be changed to suit differing contexts while the identity remains the same.

Famous brands such as Renault, who for many years used the melody from Robert Palmer's 'Johnny & Mary' as their sonic logo, created more than 150 different arrangements for different advertising campaigns all over Europe. British Airways (BA), who for nearly 15 years have used the melody of the 'Flower Duet' from the opera *Lakme* by Delibes, have had more than 20 arrangements created. In some cases, as with their award-winning UK radio commercial 'India', the music has been arranged in such a way as to make the choice of instruments the very essence of the message. In this specific case, using a piano and sitar to convey the fact that BA flies to India.

In both these cases, the melody has remained distinct and consistent, so the identity has remained consistent. At the same time, the arrangements have changed, flexing to suit specific contexts, giving the sonic identity a freedom not always enjoyed by graphic or linguistic elements.

Honest

In this context, honesty really means 'on-brand' and as such is at the heart of branding. Like the other criteria that define successful branding, being 'on-brand' is tricky to define, primarily because it is judged emotionally. There are no mathematical formulae beyond the mathematics of aesthetics but honest branding just feels right. It fits emotionally and aesthetically with every component and every brand association, for every stakeholder. It just *is*.

Part two: conclusion

We now have a model for brands and a set of criteria for branding, which is the expression of a brand. It is within this context that sonic branding comes to life and we can see where sound and music in particular can play a great role in the fundamental process. To recap: the dominant and most influential understanding of brands today is that they are, in essence, beliefs that form the basis for ideas.

The fundamental task of those who seek to turn these ideas into tangible brands involves generating belief in others. To do this, the new ideas must be different to the old and must be identified as such, primarily through names, symbols and value. Furthermore, they must at some stage offer benefits, either functional or emotional, to their stakeholders. Stakeholders must trust a brand and believe in its reliability. Brands encourage this through consistency, which is of the essence of the brand experience movement where every time a stakeholder comes into contact with a brand, the experience is consistent with the belief, idea and values.

To be a brand today and in the future, brands must consider their sustainability, which is a function of a brand's positive emotions, finances and the effectiveness with which feedback is handled by the brand. Armed with an understanding for the building blocks of sonic branding; sound and brands, we can now investigate a model for how some more brands have successfully brought the two together to enhance their communications. The model we will present is Sonicbrand's own; to some this extent represents the 'family jewels' of the business ...

PART 3

This is How We Do It

By now, the associations between people, sound and brands should be obvious. With this in mind, we now turn our attention to establishing a model of how to create sonic branding that will enable a brand to communicate its emotional values and generate belief amongst stakeholders. Sonicbrand was formed because the model for how to do this did not exist, despite the obvious desire of brand-owners to use the touchpoints available to them in the most effective way. Of course, there were and remain many different businesses in the related areas of branding and musical composition. Unfortunately, they had never really spoken to each other and had never developed a workable process for creating sonics that could be used consistently over time and media.

My work, together with Paul and Ali, has been to understand the issues of branding with sound and discover new ways to harness the many opportunities that they present. Primarily, the aim of the business is to build a consistent approach to sound that enhances the ability of each individual touchpoint to convey its part of the brand's distinct belief and values. The overarching principle of our approach is collaboration. It is only by working in harness with brand-owners and their many creative agencies that we can deliver the most relevant and resonant strategy and creative work.

In the past, brand-owners have been kept at arms length from composers by the main intermediary, the ad agency. This has suited agency and composer alike as they have kept their creative secrets to themselves and maintained a kind of price-fixing cartel. Today, as brand-owners become less reliant on their lead ad agency, they see the value of working directly with all those who can help them learn about and express their brands. In most cases, the extra effort to get involved directly with sonic branding is rewarded with better, more resonant creative work and lower long-term costs for licences.

The case studies detailed within this section will demonstrate how talented people have collaborated to harness some of the potential of sonic branding in one medium or another. Very few have ever managed to use sound effectively across all their media channels and the main reason has been a lack of willingness to collaborate. Rather than focus on why consistent sonic branding has been so rare, however, we will focus on how to make more of it in the future.

CHAPTER 16

The sonic branding engine

What we will seek to do in the chapters ahead is generate a model that can be referenced by anyone who wants to make full use of sound as a brand communicator. We call this the sonic branding engine and it is the heart of our strategic approach. Even more important in sonic branding terms than the sheer creativity of musical or effects composition, it represents the essence of the sonic branding approach.

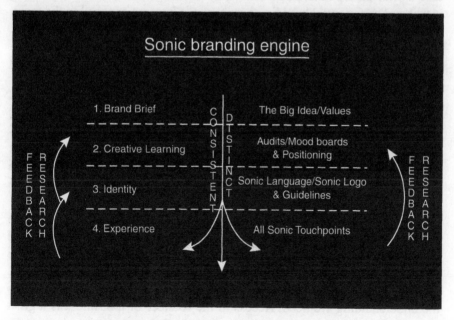

Figure 16.1 The sonic branding engine

CHAPTER 17

Brand brief

In creating our model, we drew heavily upon our experiences in different realms of communications and creativity. Paul's training and career in advertising, in particular, were extremely useful in giving Sonicbrand an understanding of the importance of the creative brief to any project. Getting the right brief is half the battle. We realized quickly too that in order to build sonics from a brand perspective, with the flexibility to work across all platforms and media through time, we would have to start with a very solid understanding of the brand before we got near to the creative work itself.

Luckily, we were not the first business that needed to establish how to take a brief on the nature of a brand. By working with the world's leading visual and experiential branding agencies, we became exposed to the many ways in which graphic and 3D design are briefed from a brand perspective. Igor Stravinsky once said that a good composer does not imitate; he steals. I like to think that what we did was steal the best bits of everyone else's brand-briefing process and apply them to our needs.

We need the brand brief to inform our creative work and make it consistent with everything else that the brand puts out as touchpoints. With it, we can generate consistency and, though it is sometimes a long and drawn-out process, the long-term reward for getting it right at this stage is that it enables the rest of the process to move more smoothly. Specifically, the brand brief involves the brand guardians imparting their knowledge of the central belief or big idea of the brand. Certain scenarios facilitate this.

The easiest scenario for us involves small or young organizations where the founders are still in charge and very much in touch with why they started the brand in the first place. In such a case, the brand guardians tend to have very detailed emotional understanding of the brand and its central belief. Interrogation of staff members is usually very rewarding and gives us the understanding we need. Access to the founder of a business is a great privilege because it can save a huge amount of time that might have to be spent digging for belief. In some cases, for example working with Imparo (a start-up educational software business), a single meeting with the founder and his closest team has proved sufficient to provide all the insight we required to understand the brand. Having founders or top executives handle the briefing process also has dividends down the line in areas such as creative sign-off.

Where brand guardians have called upon the services of a strategic branding agency such as Landor or Enterprise IG before addressing sonics, the central belief of the brand is almost always clearly visible in the work that these agencies carry out. As a result, access to documents such as the brand guidelines can give us additional information to supplement the discussion sessions that must inevitably take place. Written documents can never be the only source of a brand brief as they are often open to wide interpretation but they give great clues to the formal nature of the brand. They also demonstrate how the brand is already interpreted graphically. Visual branding has many parallels with sonic branding and by viewing logos, fonts, shapes and colours, we can be inspired regarding the sonic interpretations yet to come.

The Royal Institution of Chartered Surveyors

The more challenging scenarios involve brands whose success has given them size and heritage but little link back to the original motivations of the brand. A fine example of a client like this is the Royal Institution of Chartered Surveyors (RICS). It is a trade body and regulator of some centuries' standing whose size and royal charter has long since overshadowed the original beliefs of the organization. In fact, when we started working with them in 2000, they had only recently acknowledged that RICS was a brand and should be treated as such.

We were employed by the design department and as such had no access to the top executives of the institution. Indeed, it seemed to us that very few people had access to the top executives. The result of the absence of a central power from our process was that every individual we encountered had a very different and personal perspective on RICS and some were still reluctant to talk about it in terms of brand at all. The task to establish the central belief of the brand, therefore, required us first to assemble a representative group of RICS staff and through a series of workshops, help them establish what the brand meant and stood for. The workshops were discussion sessions, where music was used to stimulate the conversation. The group, which had members of mixed musical, brand, marketing and surveying experience was able to react to the musical stimuli in a broadly uniform way and use pieces of music to express how they and their constituency felt about the brand.

Over a period of some months, we were able to give the group the confidence to express itself and define the essence of the brand. The composition of the group was very important, as it included representatives from many different departments within RICS, not just design or marketing. Brands belong to all their stakeholders, as discussed in earlier chapters, so it is vital to canvass as many opinions as possible. Probably the most useful member of the RICS team was the call centre manager who had more day to day exposure to the RICS members than anyone else. She was able to give unique insight into how the institution was perceived and what might be expected from it in the future. The call centre manager may not be on every brand task force but one never knows who within an organization is going to have the most insightful view of the brand. Often we have found that those outside of the marketing function can bring some unexpected and important perspective that shapes the whole process.

Within the brand brief, alongside the big idea lies the value set of the organization. This, as we know, is a vital component of the brand and therefore becomes an equally important component of the sonic branding process. In most cases, it is the value set that informs the greatest part of the creative work to come and it is, therefore, extremely useful for an organization to already have its values well defined and in place before approaching sonic branding.

Vizzavi (part 1)

When working with Vizzavi (a start-up electronic and mobile communications company, founded by Vodafone and Vivendi and later a great casualty of the burst Dotcom bubble), we were exposed to a set of values right at the start of our work. This was very helpful as it gave us a quick and easy way to approach the emotional context of the brand. These original values were:

- Soft technology
- Modern heritage
- Human energy
- Social.

Each value was backed up by a secondary set of descriptors or defining phrases that put flesh on the bones. Thus, 'soft technology' referred to the desire to deliver technology in a human way and 'modern heritage' referred to the founding companies' experience in delivering cutting-edge services. Human energy and social were a little more self-explanatory.

Even though the value set continued to evolve as the business moved from start-up to launch, the original values gave a foundation for all our work with the brand. They also formed the criteria by which the sonic branding could be judged. If the value set is well established and understood then the sonic branding can be evaluated in terms of how well it communicates these values. This gives us a huge advantage, as it takes a big slice of personal subjectivity out of the process later on. Personal subjectivity or taste is not the enemy of a sonic branding project, which relies upon gut-feel, but it can become harmful if allowed to run unchecked. We have witnessed the process for selecting sonics for a single brand takes years as a result of opposing personal tastes overriding what is right for expressing the brand values.

CHAPTER 18

Creative learning

The brand brief gives us an understanding of the brand, primarily through the verbal expressions of staff and the graphic and written expressions contained in documents. The next stage, creative learning, is where we truly start to uncover how the brand will eventually express itself in sound. We do this through a series of audits and group discussions of sonic moodboards.

Historical audit

As we saw in the first two sections, sound has been used for many years by many great brands, but in reality all brands already express themselves in sound. The vast majority have made no impact on their audiences because they have missed the crucial points of consistency over time and across touchpoints but even the most seemingly silent brands communicate through sound somewhere.

The first step in the creative learning stage involves listening to the brand's pre-existing sonic touchpoints. These will obviously vary by brand but can include historic approaches to advertising, telephone hold systems, office music, events or corporate videos. Wherever it may be, we always uncover some heritage, even if it is best forgotten. Sometimes though, the historical audit throws up some interesting, remarkable or even breakthrough information and even the most seemingly quiet brands can sometimes have a rich heritage in the use of voice or music. Music on a corporate film, for example, may have been absolutely spot-on for a brand but because of the way the project was undertaken or the cost of licensing the track, it will have become lost in the history of the brand.

The historical audit will uncover a brand's own instinctive approach to sonics and use it as a reference for the future, consistent approach that will be implemented. Occasionally, it will even throw up a sonic branding property right under the noses of the brand guardians and when it does, it shows how uncovering a brand's sonic heritage can be incredibly powerful for helping brand guardians to realize just how important sonic branding has been in the past for their brand.

When working recently for BP, we uncovered some sonic branding for one of their most respected sub-brands; Castrol GTX. Throughout the 1970s and 1980s, Castrol used a single piece of music consistently in its advertising. Even hearing it today makes me remember the ads with the oil running down the side of the can. Despite this, the BP folk, when asked if the corporation had any sonic branding gave a resounding no, until they were reminded of the sonic branding that their 1970s ad agency had provided for them. This discovery added much weight and reassurance to the sonic branding process and really brought home how powerful sonics can be.

BMW (GB)

Another example of a brand that did not realize it owned sonic branding until it tried to change it is BMW (GB) Limited. Below, Paul Fulberg explains his drive into the heart of their sonic branding.

With experience becoming the new buzz word of branding it is worth reminding ourselves that for some brands, experience is and always has been part of the product itself. A great example of this is cars. Every time you sit in a car you are not just driving from A to B, you are interacting with a brand. You are able to touch, see, smell and hear the brand, you are not yet able to taste it but I am not sure if there will ever be need to taste a dashboard. Cars are products that immerse you in a brand and everything it stands for.

In August 2002, I interviewed Phil Horton, the marketing director of BMW (GB), in order to learn how his brand communicates the values behind its propeller logo through traditional media and the cars themselves. Earlier in 2002, I had discussed the brand with Tim Greenhill of Greenhill McCarron Ltd, a design agency that had worked with BMW for many years. He had given us a little insight into the importance of sound in all aspects of BMW's brand communications and experience so I was keen to learn more.

At a car manufacturer every employee from the boardroom to the factory floor has the role of brand guardian. Car brands are not just about logos, colour schemes and corporate guidelines. They are about every detail that makes up their products. In these moving brand identities, sound plays as important a role as the way in which the gear-stick slips into gear every time or the glow of the dashboard at night.

At BMW they fully appreciate this and, like many other car manufacturers, have invested heavily in sound engineering. As Horton said, in reference to sound, when

I spoke with him, 'There is more that we are doing with the cars now than we have ever done before'. He is not exaggerating. Every sound made by a BMW is analysed by a team of over 200 acoustic engineers to ensure they are both mechanically and aesthetically correct. The doors have a reassuringly solid sound as they close, the buttons click with purpose and the dashboard remains silent whatever the driving conditions. Then of course there is the main sound producer, the engine. BMW have to live up to the fact that they are known as a luxury sports saloon manufacturer, and therefore have to ensure their cars sound sporty while keeping engine noise to a desirable level. Achieving this balance is both complex and expensive but if the brand experience is to be right the expense is well worth it.

With car manufacturers making such a huge investment in sound from a product perspective you would expect there to be an equal level of importance placed upon it in the marketing communications. Unfortunately, in most cases this is not the case. There are some classic examples of automotive sonic branding. You read earlier how Oldsmobile was probably the first with its song, 'In my merry Oldsmobile', which became an American advertising icon. More recently we have heard Renault's consistent use of the Robert Palmer track, 'Johnny and Mary', for their Clio advertising in the UK. By the time the Clio's advertising concept had run its course in 1997 over 150 versions of the track are believed to have been produced to cover all possible contexts. So do BMW utilize the power of sonic branding in their marketing communications? Well since Phil Horton used to be the marketing and communications director at Renault, UK, you will not be surprised to hear that the answer is yes.

Let me give you a bit of background about the BMW brand in the UK before we explore why a single voice has been able to encompass everything that the brand stands for. BMW was founded in Germany in 1916 as an aircraft engine manufacturer, which explains its propeller logo with sky blue colouring. It began building bikes in 1923 and then moved into cars in 1926. Today, BMW mainly produces cars and motorbikes which are critically acclaimed and sold the world over.

In order to exercise greater control of the brand and the distribution of its products, BMW set up a UK office about 25 years ago. From the very beginning BMW understood the importance of establishing a clear understanding of what its brand stood for in the UK and communicating this clearly. So with the help of WCRS, who are still their advertising agency today, BMW (GB), identified the following set of core brand values: quality, technology, exclusivity and performance. Over time the brand positioning has evolved but the four core values have remained the same. In fact, in 25 years the only major addition to the BMW brand positioning has been a focus on driveability which is now articulated through their marketing communications strap-line, 'The Ultimate Driving Machine'. This loyalty to the core values demonstrates how the BMW brand has been built on consistency, a fact that later proved crucial in establishing their sonic brand identity.

Car advertising is said to fulfil two roles. As you can probably work out for yourself the first role is as a sales tool, encouraging consumers to select a certain brand and model. The second role is to reassure those who have already bought a brand that they have made the right decision. It is quite easy to do this in a visual medium as often the image of the car itself can do everything for you, but in an audio only medium, like radio, you have to be more creative. Radio is a widely considered to be an excellent medium for selling cars, for one reason in particular – you can reach people while they are sitting in them. Add to this the fact that it is a great medium for advertisers due to its low cost relative to other media, and you have a very strong argument for making it a key part of a car brand's media strategy. With this in mind, BMW decided to develop a brand campaign for radio.

BMW needed a radio campaign that communicated their distinct view of their core brand values. WCRS' response was a number of concepts that seemed to be the audio equivalent of the BMW visual style. The ads were basically a voiceover informing the listener of the various technical and aesthetic benefits of BMW engineering. The voiceover needed to be mature and calm in order to allow the listener time to take in and contemplate the information being read to them while at the same time appealing to the ear of the BMW customer.

To make sure the radio concepts fulfilled their aims, WCRS undertook some prelaunch consumer research. They played groups of consumers the radio treatments read by a number of different voiceovers, including David Suchet who had voiced the brand's TV advertising for over ten years. The results proved very interesting in the search for the right sound and feel for the ads. They showed that BMW had organically developed a sonic brand identity and that without it the radio ads would struggle to fulfil their aims. Their identity is not a logo, a piece of music or a sound effect, it was a voice. To be specific it is the voice of David Suchet, a British actor better known for his portrayal of Agatha Christie's Poirot in the TV series of the same name. The intelligent selection of Suchet to be the voiceover on BMW's TV advertising ten years earlier, when combined with their consistent use of him, had created an effective sonic brand identity. I'll let Phil Horton explain:

> David [Suchet]'s voice, although subtle, proved to be very much a BMW property, part of our sonic branding, in fact probably the only sonic branding we have. The qualitative research shows that it does work, even stronger than we thought; over time he has become associated with BMW.[1]

What of the rest of the sonic components in the ads? Originally the soundtracks for the ads were going to be quite obvious ambient sounds. However, when the creative team were in the studio it became apparent that if these were too loud in the mix they would detract from the strength of Suchet's voice. In the words of Horton, 'It is important to give his voice room to breathe during the ads.' Finally the correct mix for the voiceover and soundtrack was found and the ads were finalized.

The whole process proved educational for both BMW (GB) and WCRS as they both learned the value of sonic branding. BMW had discovered its sonic self and realized how it adds a whole new dimension to their brand communications. Without the brand associations provided by Suchet's voice, BMW would have been less inclined to use radio and would therefore have been unable to take advantage of the benefits it offers.

Competitive audit

The second audit takes in the competitive landscape. As we showed in Chapter 15, distinctiveness is one of the four aims of any brand. In order to ensure that we are going to be creating sonic branding that really is distinct, we need to listen to what is already out there and make sure that we do not sound anything like it.

The most useful resources for the competitive audit are archives of old advertising. These are easily accessed and can give us decades of material to study. Most competitive audits usually underline just how inconsistent brands and their advertising agencies have been in regard to their sonics, which in itself opens up the opportunity to create distinctiveness merely through consistency.

Some marketplaces are already dominated by established sonic branding. BA, as the national carrier and owner of some of the best sonic branding around, was the dominant airline advertiser of the 1980s and 1990s. When Go, the low-cost airline, came along, its radio advertising strategy dictated that sonic branding should be developed. Because there was already a consistent player in the market, it had to find a creative rather than strategic route to distinctiveness. It did this through clever composition that was then applied consistently and in doing so gave us one of our best case studies. Below, Paul Fulberg recounts one of the classic sonic branding stories.

A tale of two airlines

When it comes to consistency in sonic branding terms there are very few global companies that can hold a candle to 'the world's favourite airline'. Few brand-owners really understand the power of sound in the same way as British Airways (BA) and even they didn't fully appreciate it until quite recently. In 2000 when BA decided to dispense with its sonic heritage, in an attempt to rebrand itself as the airline for the twenty-first century, it was not long before they discovered that they had thrown the baby out with the bathwater.

Leo Delibes' 'Flower Duet' from the opera *Lakme* was a little-known piece until the advertising agency Saatchi and Saatchi, with the help of the infamous but brilliant director Tony Kaye, created the BA 'Eye' television commercial. The ad was a huge success and BA used it, unchanged, for many years. Even when the visuals were replaced the music played on. BA had harnessed the power of sound and whether by accident or design they had created a new level to their brand identity.

It wasn't long before BA realized that their sonic branding could be used in any medium that could deliver sound and Delibes' beautiful piece was soon being heard on BA planes all over the world, in airport shuttles at Heathrow, on the hold system of the call centre and on radio as well as TV advertising. Wherever and whenever BA's customers came into contact with the brand there was an opportunity to immerse them in everything the brand stood for.

All of this is very interesting but BA's sonic branding does have one fundamental flaw – it doesn't belong to them. Leo Delibes wrote *Lakme* in 1883 and died eight years later. Copyright law protects a work for 70 years after which time it becomes public property. By the time BA had discovered the magic of the 'Flower Duet' it was well and truly in the public domain. Although they could protect the actual versions they used, BA could not stop anyone else from using the piece itself. A key part of branding, no matter who you ask, is that it must be ownable.

BA couldn't copyright or trademark the Flower Duet and literally had to wait and see if anyone else decided to use the piece. Eventually someone did. In 1998 Ford launched the Galaxy, their people carrier, in the UK. The most important thing they wanted to communicate about the new car was that it is so luxurious and spacious that it can make you feel like you are travelling first class. What better way to do this than to pretend that the people in the ad are travelling in the first class cabin of a plane and what better music to use than Delibes' 'Flower Duet'.

As BA were unable to control the use of their sonic brand identity, Ford were able to use the 'Flower Duet' and in so doing borrow all the brand values that had become associated with the track through years of investment. Rumour has it that Ford asked for permission at the highest level before proceeding with the advertising campaign but they did so out of courtesy rather than necessity. In this case BA was lucky as the Ford ad was a positive association. The lack of ownership, however, means there is nothing to stop one of BA's competitors using the track in a derogatory way.

In 2000 when BA chose to abandon Delibes in the search for a more modern image they turned to the rather literal 'Something in the Air' written by John Keen. It was a modern track, compared to Delibes, with lyrics that talked of revolution and suggested that the brand was more about flower-power than flower duets. Consumers may have liked the track in its own right, but it did not say BA to them and after the most catastrophic event in air travel history, 11 September, they were looking for what they knew and trusted rather than the latest thing. In a quite impressive U-turn, BA returned to Delibes and even apologized on their corporate website for ever taking it away! Despite this blip, BA has been extremely consistent with its sonic branding over the last couple of decades – one can ignore their little mistake in 2000 – and has created a property that is probably more powerful than their visual symbols.

BA is not alone in the airline world in providing us with a great real-world example of the power of consistently used sonic branding. Interestingly, it is a company born of BA that is our other example; this one is perhaps more notable because it set out on a conscious quest for sonic branding and created its own.

Go was set up in 1998 as a response to the arrival of BA's new arch nemesis, easyJet. The age of the low-cost airline had arrived and easyJet was destroying the traditional airlines on their short-haul routes by offering no-frills travel at no-frills prices. Go was BA's version of a low-cost airline which meant it had to have the style and quality of its parent without the expense.

Go's marketing director, David Magliano, sought to create a brand that combined quality with fun and low costs. This was very much evident in the brand identity created by a Wolff Olins team under the command of Doug Hamilton, the man most credited for the Orange identity. Go's colourful, two-dimensional visual identity combined with its no-nonsense name made the brand stand out from the crowd. It was both stylish and simple, it said everything that needed to be said about the company. But for Magliano there was something missing from the identity and he knew exactly what it was.

It will become clear to you what was missing when you learn that Magliano's first job in advertising was as an executive working on the Kwik-Fit account, the Ford-owned car servicing business. Kwik-Fit will always be remembered in the UK for its unforgettable jingle: 'You Can't Get Better Than A Kwik-Fit Fitter'. It wasn't the kind of jingle that you'd find yourself humming in the bath but as soon as you heard the first couple of notes on an ad you knew what was coming. Another thing about David Magliano that may give you a clue is that his favourite media is radio, in his words: 'I love radio. Radio is a lovely medium, I love its intimacy.'[2]

Having developed the visual identity with Wolff Olins, Go turned to Howell Henry Chaldecott Lury (HHCL), one of the UK's leading ad agencies, to help them develop an advertising strategy that would allow them to achieve high brand awareness and product understanding in a very short amount of time. It was decided that the best way to do this was to take the corporate identity and feed it to the public through the advertising. The launch campaign was simple and direct but it lacked a strong audio element. It is at this point that we'll let Magliano take over the story.

We were faced with a blank canvas when it came to sound so the first thing we did was use known voiceovers on the advertising, we used John Hannah to start with. We then discovered the disadvantage of using John in that he started filming *The Mummy Returns* and was no longer available. So we switched to the guy from *Cold Feet* [TV drama series], James Nesbitt.

I quite like the use of a soft regional accent. You talk about emotional fit; well at the time we were trying to establish the Go brand as a professional, reliable and established airline. The soft male regional voiceover seemed to give this image. I can't remember for certain but I'm sure there was some kind of ambient music bed on the ads.

Having successfully launched the brand through a variety of media and achieved impressive levels of brand recognition Go now needed to achieve long-term success. In order to achieve this in the low-cost air travel sector, Go had to be able to ensure there was constant demand for seats. Air travel companies are faced with the fact that they have a 'fixed perishable inventory' – each company will have a certain number of planes with a certain number of seats. Every time a plane takes off with empty seats the possible income from those seats is lost forever. Faced with this fact, it was important that Go had a media and creative strategy that allowed them to quickly react to forthcoming periods of low demand, which they might not know about more then five weeks in advance.

The ideal media for such a reactive market are press and radio. In the press it is relatively easy to develop a template for an ad into which you can simply drop new information. Radio is not quite as simple. Radio is a very transient media; it is important to capture people's attention, tell them all you want to tell them and then leave them with a memory. There is no chance for the listener to rewind. So how can you give a listener a lot of quite dry information in a way that will not only capture their attention but also leave them with a memory of the brand and the offer?

In most cases a creative agency will search for an interesting, often humorous, concept that will entertain the listener. This method, although superb when you have a set product with a set time frame, is not so good when a lot of your advertising is spur-of-the-moment stuff. What Go needed was an audio template for their radio ads and in order to create this a sonic brand identity more unique than a celebrity voiceover was required. Back to Magliano.

> So I asked HHCL to develop some form of sonic branding to make us stand out. Given our sector we could not spend large amounts of time or money on advertising production so we needed a mechanism, an audio template, that would allow us to quickly and clearly communicate route and offer information. I didn't want to have to spend two or three days coming up with some witty ad execution.

And so the creative process for the Go sonic brand identity began. It was a long process, the exact length of which is unknown, but it took somewhere between one and two years to achieve a piece of music that did everything that was required of it.

> HHCL worked with a number of composers and we reviewed a lot of material. We would listen to a lot of tracks but as I lacked the vocabulary to be able to communicate effectively with the composers, 'this one isn't right' didn't seem to be very productive feedback.
>
> There was one piece that we listened to that seemed to be right. It had an ambling rhythm and quite subtly included airport sound effects. But it felt a bit literal. It was simply a music bed rather than a piece of branding. Then at one meeting HHCL presented a piece that they thought was fun but they didn't expect us to like. From the first time I heard it I liked it. It had the right emotional fit. In sound terms it was everything that the visual identity was. It didn't have a huge amount of depth or complexity, you didn't need to 'get it'.

Magliano knew he had a very powerful brand communications property when he heard the Go sonic identity for the first time. He knew that with this happy, easy-listening piece of music as a backdrop he could give the consumer some very dry information about new routes or offers without the consumer ignoring it. He also knew that even if the listener didn't take in all the information they would at least pick up some of the brand values. And so the template was established; a short intro, a space for a voiceover, a chorus of 'Go Go Go Go Go' and then a finale. It doesn't sound a lot but it worked and it worked well. New ads could be produced very quickly, the listener was told everything they needed to know and best of all they stood out from all the other ads around them.

One thing that Magliano was keen to ensure was that the brand did not suffer from listener fatigue. With 23% of the media budget being spent on radio, listeners of commercial radio were never far from hearing a Go advertisement. HHCL were asked to explore ways of further developing the sonic identity in order to keep it fresh. Having established a very strong sonic brand language with the vocal element and the emotion being at the forefront, any composer charged with moving the identity on had a great deal of flexibility to work with. Their response was to experiment with different genres which originated from Go's destinations. They created a variety of versions that were not simple rearrangements of the core brand identity. The existence of a strong sonic language meant that as long as the pieces had certain features they could be as different as they liked, for example a salsa version was created. These new versions extended the brand identity but also communicated information about the offer being explained in the voiceover.

The radio campaign was incredibly successful and combined with the other media allowed Go to become the second largest low-cost airline in the UK carrying 4.3 million passengers in 2001. But advertising was not the only place where the Go sonic branding showed its worth. In a lesson learnt from their parent company they also made sound part of the whole travel experience. As with BA, the Go theme could be heard on the flights and the airport shuttles. The happy feeling of the music helped make the Go experience more pleasurable while at the same time reinforcing the identity that passengers had got to know through the advertising. Due to the easy-listening style of the core sonic brand identity, the music proved to be unintrusive enough to make it a pleasant backdrop to the travel experience. In the words of one consumer, 'You don't realise how infectious it is until you start singing along. It's brilliant'.[3]

It would have been easy for Go to have plastered their sonic brand identity everywhere but they understood the importance of creating a complete brand experience rather than just a world of advertising. This lead to a considered approach to the use of the sonic identity; time, place and audience were all taken into account for its implementation. A good example of this was the fact that flight crews were given control of the music and allowed to determine themselves if the music would be welcome in the plane. In some cases, such as early morning flights where the passengers were mainly businessmen, it was considered better to have silence. In other areas such as the call centres the core music was not thought to be suitable and therefore a special arrangement was planned.

All this adds up to one of the most effective examples of sonic branding that has ever been undertaken in the commercial environment. Go unfortunately is no more and the identity is probably lost forever but this was not due to commercial failure. In fact Go proved so successful that in 2002 it was bought by its main competitor, easyJet. David Magliano is now the marketing director of easyJet and I'm sure it will not be long before he releases his passion for sonic branding on the orange colossus of low-cost air travel.

UK food retail

The competitive audit can also give brands extra impetus for investment in sonic branding. If we briefly examine extracts from a competitive audit of the UK food retailing sector, we can see how some interesting insights into the nature of the businesses themselves can be uncovered.

Of the top four supermarkets in the UK – Tesco, Sainsbury, ASDA and Safeway – only Safeway does not employ sonic branding techniques in its communications. This despite it owning one of the most memorable jingles in UK advertising history 'Safeways, everything you want from a store and a little bit more.'

Sainsbury has a bizarre approach to sonic branding, using it solely for its radio advertising and leaving the choice of music on TV ads and in-store largely to chance and personal choices. This seems to be ignoring the fact that the same people listen to the radio as watch TV and visit the stores. Any simple evaluation of the customer journey through the day will demonstrate that, as a result of the mixed strategy, the customer will be getting mixed messages which cannot help the brand communicate its beliefs.

Tesco, despite owning a simple sonic logo, uses it only sporadically. The reasons for this are not clear but the unsophisticated nature of the property may be to blame. There has been little thought given to the need for flexibility or the ability for sonic logos to change and adapt to suit their context. Additionally, in owning only a logo, Tesco does not have any identity elements that can be used across touchpoints such as in-store or on the phone.

Finally, the rise and rise of ASDA throughout the 1990s was made possible by clever management, the everyday low prices strategy and some extremely powerful advertising that was dominated by sonic branding that survives in an updated form today. The brand advertising, created by Publicis in the UK, used a simple, cheap and cheerful melody that had a perfect emotional fit with the low-price positioning. Added to the melody was the simple sonic and graphic device of a housewife patting the copious amount of coins in her back pocket that represented the savings she had made thanks to ASDA.

At the same time as this advertising was generating impact through the touchpoints of TV and radio, ASDA started its own in-store radio station to make full and strategic use of sound within the store environment. Though far from unique as a concept, what made ASDA radio so interesting were the links formed between the in-store medium and the media planning and buying for the advertising, held by TMD Carat at the time. ASDA utilized the radio expertise of their media-planning agency to help formulate programming and advertising strategies in-store that were consistent with messages through external media.

As a result of the ASDA case study, we now have a working model for the sonic strategies of our client that could have taken far longer to formulate were it not for the competitive audit.

Contextual audit

The final audit is of the various touchpoints or contexts, where the sonic branding will eventually be employed. Primarily, the audit gives us a chance to uncover new opportunities for sonic branding that may not have previously been considered. This audit also allows us to become familiar with the specific technical and creative issues that relate to each context for brand communications.

IVRs, for example, offer limited quality playback that needs special consideration. Retail environments have varying acoustic qualities which need to be understood, as do the feelings of the staff who work there with regard to the use of sound. In fact, the contextual audit allows us to meet all the teams of people who control the content and delivery of every touchpoint. This gives us the opportunity to explain the overall goals of the sonic branding project as well as hear the specific needs of every context.

CHAPTER 19

Moodboards

With the audits completed, we usually have plenty of reference materials to fuel the next part of the process. The backgrounds that Paul and I have in advertising and the media led us to believe that there were great benefits to using visual moodboards as an aid to a visual brief. When describing any creative guide, it is almost always useful to use stimuli other than the written and spoken word to give ideas form. Similarly, our backgrounds in music and theatre taught us that creating demo tracks or listening to pre-existing music with the intention of learning from the most appropriate pieces were very strong steps towards the creation of great music and design in sound. Bringing together this knowledge, Sonicbrand developed a creative process around sonic moodboards.

There are two types of moodboard that we use at Sonicbrand. The first is the 'big idea' or 'belief' moodboard. Like any visual moodboard, this is a collection of reference materials that approaches the central belief or idea of the brand in varying ways. In the visual world, I have seen moodboards covered with anything from beads to fake fur, carpets and pictures from magazines or logos from cars or supermarkets. There has also, among the larger visual branding agencies been a move in recent years towards the 'living' or video moodboard, whereby film stock, music and sound effects are mixed together to form a moodboard with movement and dynamism. Jon Turner introduced this approach to Enterprise IG, the WPP-owned brand consultants. There is validity in the living moodboard for sonic branding briefs but we have found the visual context they present to be distracting, particularly when entirely non-visual touchpoints such as the radio have been identified for inclusion in the branding.

As a result, in the sonic world, the reference material for moodboards is entirely audio and is dominated by the use of music that has been composed to convey an overall emotion or belief that is similar to that of the brand. There is such a broad range of music available today that almost any situation has already been composed for. Thus, we rely upon our knowledge of what is out there to select the right pieces for any one moodboard.

Of course, a vast and well-referenced music library is a great help as is the encyclopaedic musical knowledge of individuals within Sonicbrand.

A particularly rich seam of material is the vast archive of film scores that have been created over the last 75 years. If one considers just how many scenes have had music written specifically for them, it is easy to imagine that almost every emotion has been tackled musically in the cinema. From Charlie Chaplin's own compositions for the 1931 movie *City Lights* to Badly Drawn Boy's 2002 scoring of Nick Hornby's *About a Boy*, the vast output of Hollywood, and indeed Bollywood, has created as rich and diverse a selection of reference material as could ever be imagined. It is possible to argue that the finest composers of the twentieth century expressed themselves primarily through movie music; Max Steiner in the 1930s and 1940s was responsible for the themes to *Gone with the Wind* and *Casablanca*, for example. Elmer Bernstein created true classics in the scores for *The Magnificent Seven* and *The Great Escape*. Henry Mancini expressed the essence of *The Pink Panther* more eloquently in his theme tune than any other component of the film managed. John Barry (*Zulu, Midnight Cowboy*), Ennio Morricone (*The Mission, Cinema Paradiso*), Bernard Herrmann (*Taxi Driver, Psycho*) and John Williams (*Star Wars, Schindler's List*) can be listed among the truly great composers of the last century. They are responsible in so many ways for how we experience the movies and for the great emotional impact the medium has on its audiences.

Every film score, of course, is different and every moodboard is distinct and new in its own way too. The choice of reference materials evolves throughout the briefing and auditing stages. It starts from as broad a base and range of styles as possible. Every piece of music ever written is a candidate. From there a narrowing and refinement takes place as pieces with the right emotion are retained and moved forward as pieces that do not fit the brand are discarded. Eventually, a moodboard that closely reflects the central belief of the brand is assembled. It will ideally consist of eight or more pieces that aggregate to express the big idea in its entirety. Each individual component, however, can never be perfect on its own as every piece of music has been written for a context or purpose that is different to that of the brand.

It is always important to have a number of pieces in the moodboard for another reason. When presented as a direction for musical creative work, a single piece of music can often be latched onto by the decision makers for a project. Once established as the 'ideal' piece within their minds, it is hard for the piece to be replaced, no matter how good the new composition may be. This scenario will be familiar to anyone who has ever presented creative work of any kind that was accompanied by a single piece of 'guide' music.

It is common practice in advertising agencies to present 'animatics', the sketch stage of TV commercials, to their client with a hastily chosen musical accompaniment. On many occasions these tracks, to nobody's great advantage, end up being used for the final commercial because they have become lodged in the client's psyche.

In many ways, once the ear and mind link a piece of music with a visual context it is almost impossible to separate them again. Thus, to escape this potential straitjacket, we always have a number of different pieces of reference music at this early stage. Two example moodboards are shown below.

Sample moodboard 1: Guardian Unlimited is the online arm of *The Guardian* newspaper, a UK national daily with a serious, left-wing style. Its brand mixes contemporary values with those of trust and heritage. The moodboard tries to capture these values in varying styles.

Sample moodboard 2: The Big Bus, a children's educational web and CD ROM application.

These two disparate examples are moodboards created to reflect the belief and values of the brands in their entirety. They are belief or big idea moodboards, seeking to convey the overall emotions of the brands and act as a beacon for the creative journey. In many cases, the big idea moodboard is all that is required before we undertake creative work. For example, Imparo, the owners of The Big Bus were very much 'big idea' people who were happy to make decisions based primarily on instinct. Some other clients, such as Vizzavi, rely more upon their value set and demand more

Table 19.1 Sample moodboard 1

Artist	Title
Air	Ce Matin La
Nitin Sawhney	Breathing Light
Herbie Hancock	Hang Up Your Hang-ups
Simon and Garfunkel	Silent Night/7 O'clock News
Steve Reich	Nagoya Marimbas
Sonicbrand	Sound effects collection
Steve Reich	City Life
Leftfield	Afro Left
Bossa Tres	People from the Sun
Ben Folds Five	One Angry Dwarf
Ruben Blades	Viento Y Madera

Table 19.2	Sample moodboard 2
Artist	**Title**
The Simpsons	Main theme
The Tweenies	Number One
Scooby Doo	Main theme
Postman Pat	Main theme
Top Cat	Incidental theme
Teletubbies	Main theme
Barney The Dinosaur	I love you
The Jungle Book	Bare Necessities

method and rationale. In these cases, we can go deeper into the value set of the brand to create value moodboards.

These are collections of individual sounds rather than whole pieces of music. Samples of voices, instruments or ambient sounds are collected in order to show in a step-by-step way how the individual values of a brand can be conveyed. This is a more logical approach and suits clients who thrive upon detail and reductionist understanding. Each value moodboard component is a potential building block for the sonic branding and needs to represent a value of the brand while being consistent with the overall belief or big idea. This is quite a challenge but it is fascinating too as value mood-boards allow us to get under the skin of how a composer creates music sound by sound, layer by layer.

Vizzavi (part 2)

We have already described the values of Vizzavi that made up the core of our brand brief. If we take these values in turn, we can describe how value moodboards were used to uncover the sounds that could represent the brand at micro – value – level as well as at the macro – belief – level when used together.

Soft technology

The moodboard for this value sought first to define the sounds for technology and then went on to establish a 'soft' way to convey this value. For technology, the moodboard consisted of many electronic sound effects, synthesizers and contemporary drum loops. By listening and evaluating each element, it was established that the most 'Vizzavi' way to convey technology was through fast-paced drums – the sort you might hear on a hardcore drum and bass or techno track. It was considered, however, that very fast electronic drums were a little too hard and harsh, so the moodboard went on to consider how to maintain the technological feel and energy while softening things up a little and adding some humanity.

The answer, after much discussion, came from listening to a percussion moodboard, from which the decision-making group chose African percussion, including a 'talking' drum, to play the rhythm of the techno loop. Thus, 'soft technology' became a techno drum beat played with ancient African drums.

Modern heritage

This value moodboard started out trying to define the sounds of heritage. The heritage moodboard included many examples of olde-worlde music, the kind that would traditionally have been used in commercials for banks or insurance companies. Classical pieces and the classical instruments with which they are played naturally convey heritage. Again, the challenge was to find the most 'Vizzavi' sound of heritage.

After listening to many instrumental solos, we defined the strings section of an orchestra (chiefly violins and violas) as being both full of heritage and timeless. The fullness and richness of the sound of a collection of string instruments was preferred to the solo instrument because it immediately conveyed a sense of sharing and collectiveness that was in keeping with the belief behind the brand.

Even so, it was felt that a strings section on its own could be a little too conservative for the brand and the modernity of the offering needed to be conveyed. The solution was to add some synthesized pad sounds (synthesized musical textures) to the strings section. These added an electronic edge and an extra, unexpected level of interest to the strings section.

Human energy and social

We treated these elements together because they were, in relation to the brand's beliefs, inextricable. This moodboard was full of fun. To reflect the optimistic *joie de vivre* that the brand wanted, we put together a value moodboard that had groups of people making joyous sounds from clapping and stamping their feet to banging drums and giving praise.

After much discussion, it was felt that the sound of a gospel choir in full voice was the most powerful way for Vizzavi to show its human energy and demonstrate the social approach at the same time. Added to this moodboard were some sounds of vocal percussion, a little like the sounds Bobby McFerrin made famous on his hit 'Don't Worry Be Happy'. These unusual sounds created an extra level of distinctiveness to the potentially generic gospel sound.

Finally, we created a moodboard for the overall belief of the brand, which was about freedom. The expression of freedom that was chosen to fit within the context of everything else we had created was a single male voice calling out the words 'Oh Yes'. This very simple device seemed to sum up everyone's feelings for the brand and became adopted as the icon of the brand.

The Vizzavi case study, which can be heard via **www.sonicbrand.com**, is indicative of the process we go through whenever called upon to create value moodboards and use them as a basis for our creative work. We operate methodically through the thousands of recordings and samples in our library to find creative ways to express individual values. We then rely upon the workshop environment, as broadly populated as possible, to decide which sounds, rhythms, melodies or words are best for expressing the values of the brand within the context of its central belief. The approach of value moodboards and the subsequent choices and compositions that stem from it is termed sonic layering. It is a proven method for the creation of sonic branding that has many challenges and advantages.

A major challenge is for the creative director or composer to work step by step and justify their choices of sounds either rationally or emotionally at every level before the overall shape of the work is decided. Though this approach is instinctive to some composers, most work on a more complex, emotional and holistic level, conceiving music as a whole rather than layer by layer. One method is no more valid than the other and in many scenarios, it is better to let a composer create as a whole and then analyse the branding down to its individual components rather than adopt the sonic layering process of building one layer at a time. In many ways, the choice as to whether to employ sonic layering should be left to the creative, as it is they who have the task of creating a magical emotional connection with stakeholders.

Sonic layering is most often required when instincts are deemed insufficient but that is not an indictment of the composer. Many people demand more than an instinctive approach and sonic layering allows some more rational and manageable decisions to be made rather than taking a more holistic approach. The major advantage of sonic layering is that it truly puts the decision-making group in control of the creative process as each new sound becomes accountable. This shared burden often leads to greater feelings of ownership amongst the stakeholders.

The greatest challenge is for the composer to present many options when in their creative view, a single solution seems obvious. Though a creative ego is important and desirable to some degree in all composers, it is just as important to remember that the brand's own ego must pervade and dominate all expressions, in some ways subjugating the composer to the level of arranger/producer. The brand itself should create its sonic branding. With that said, however, it is worth noting that of all the people involved in a sonic branding project, none is as well informed or instinctively aware of how to express the emotions or values of a brand as the composer. The creative's opinions must carry sufficient weight to guide the rest of the group but not to overrule them. The advantage that sonic layering gives the composer in this respect is that the step-by-step process gives the whole decision-making group the intelligence they require to know that the recommendations of the composer are probably correct.

Sonic layering, by virtue of its transparency, inherent nature and need for collaboration, is a very fast and effective way to build trust and understanding between the creative and the decision-making group. It is always viewed as optional, however, as it is time-intensive and often unnecessary when the creative's instinctive approach is already trusted.

CHAPTER 20

Identity

At the end of the moodboard workshops, we are faced with one of two scenarios. If the process is based upon big idea moodboards, then the third stage of the sonic branding engine sees the creative director armed with a musical moodboard and the feedback of the decision-making group. This feedback will have information regarding each component of the moodboard and how closely its emotions match the desired expression of the sonic branding. There will also be some detailed intelligence regarding specific instruments, rhythms or sounds that are particularly liked in the context of a brand communication.

For example, from the Big Bus moodboard outlined earlier, some of the specific feedback was that the 'sunrise' at the start of the *Teletubbies* theme was particularly consistent with the emotions of the brand and that a similar (but obviously distinct) musical device should be incorporated into the sonic branding. Similarly, the use of sound effects in the music of Steve Reich was deemed particularly relevant to the Guardian Unlimited brand's emotions. As a result, these types of sounds were carried through to the identity stage but not predefined going into that stage.

The alternative scenario, as demonstrated in the Vizzavi case study, is where the analysis of value moodboards has already given the creative director a number of clearly defined sonic layers that represent the individual values of the brand. This is the more advanced and collaborative position and it gives some strong anchor reference points for the decision-making group as the creative process continues.

As shown earlier in our examination of the nature of brands, the identity level of a brand is incredibly important because it exists at a higher level than the experience of the stakeholders and must represent the belief of the brand. Similarly, in the sonic branding engine, the identity level is the most important creatively and strategically, as the use of the sonic branding across each touchpoint gains its consistency and distinctiveness primarily as a result of how it relates back to the identity level. The identity level is primarily concerned with building a system of sonic branding that will be capable of generating the distinct, memorable, flexible and honest identifiers that a brand needs to generate belief among stakeholders. As such it is the beating heart of sonic branding.

There are a number of ways of creating the system and each one, strategically and creatively, will be different. There are some components, however, that are common to all sonic brand identities. These are the sonic language, sonic logo™ and guidelines.

CHAPTER 21

Sonic language

The visual branding world is very familiar with the concept of a language system. This would traditionally be composed of a colour palette, a font, perhaps a photographic style, layouts and shapes that are considered the language of a brand and can be used in most combinations in branded communications. In the world of sonic branding, the language system required is at least as complex, if not more so. What creates the difficulty is the fact that sound has a relationship with the passing of time that visuals, apart from film which is still rarely used in brand communications, do not share. A brochure or a press ad stands still. Sonic branding moves through time. As a result, it is much harder to define than colours or shapes. There is no set classification for sounds as yet devised because the temporal element gives sounds an infinite number of possibilities. Therefore, Sonicbrand is inventing the equivalent of a Pantone system as it goes along, though I doubt we will ever reach the point where all sounds are classified and numbered.

The sonic language aims to assemble the sounds identified during the creative process so far and express these in a clear and understandable way as the sounds that will become the cornerstones of the brand's sonic identity.

In the first case, where big idea moodboards are the only reference, it is the job of the creative director to identify the sounds that have been well received and interpret these in an ownable way. For example, where a piano melody may have been deemed on-brand, it is obvious that the piano melody reference will itself already belong to an existing piece of music. It is necessary, therefore, for the creative director to take the instrument and create a new melody that has the same emotional content as the piece referenced in the moodboard.

Exactly the same principle relates to any ambient sounds that are deemed on-brand in the big idea moodboard stage but are obviously pre-existing and subject to another's copyright. In this case, it is the job of the creative director to source and record a similar sound that can then be owned by the brand. Allowing the creative director the chance to reinterpret the brief that has come from the moodboard is a great opportunity for generating the distinctive magic that should be sought in any new music or ambient sound.

Where value moodboards have been employed, the sonic language is well defined by the time the identity stage is reached. There is less room here for interpretation of the sounds by the creative or composer but that is not to say that the creative's work is finished, far from it. The sonic language identified needs to be expressed in some way that will allow it to make sense to the decision-making group and to those who will create the brand experiences further down the line. To do this, the sonic language's temporal relationship must be expressed as must the inter-relationships of the different elements of the language. This expression usually takes the form of a brand score.

The brand score is a piece of music that brings together all the elements of the sonic language: vocal, instrumental and ambient sounds. It can vary in length, depending upon the richness of the language defined at the identity stage and will usually introduce a melody that is new, distinct, recognizable, ownable and memorable for the brand. It is in the creation of the brand score that the creative magic of music is given its chance to live. Process is what leads to an accurate brief and clear understanding of the brand but a spark is required to go from the process stage into true creativity. Brand scores, even when the sonic language has been predefined and agreed, can and should be surprising because the sonic branding must be new and distinct.

The brand score is perhaps the most important piece of the sonic branding process because it will contain all the rational and emotional information required for future sonic branding work. That said, it is not designed for use in external touchpoints for the brand. It is an expression of the sonic language in its purest form and as such has no specific reference points for the experiential contexts that apply to specific touchpoints. For example, the brand score may be three minutes in length. Simplistically, a radio ad may be 30 seconds duration or an office environment may require sonic branding for nine hours every day. Though the information required to create pieces of these varying lengths will be contained within the brand score, it in itself cannot be chopped into pieces or put on constant repeat to work fully in these scenarios. The first creative work that the brand score informs is the sonic logo. In truth, they are created simultaneously as the logo is always in the composer's mind while the brand score is designed.

There is some debate as to whether a visual logo is an intrinsic, essential part of a brand's identity and as we have discussed in Part Two of this book, some brands are starting to down-weight the importance of their logo as a way of marking themselves out from the crowds. While in the visual world, there may be some logo fatigue, it is hard to argue the same in sonics. For a start, there are still so few sonic trademarks in existence that we cannot yet be tired of them. In 2001, in the European Union Trademark Registry, there were 85,000 figurative marks registered. By contrast there were only 20 sonic marks registered and though the number of sonic marks is growing at a faster rate than visual marks, it will be some time before our heads are saturated with them.

Furthermore, an important criterion of sonic branding is that it is recognizable and memorable, even after a very short period of time. Remember that Intel's logo is less than four seconds in duration. This particular example of a sonic logo has convinced most people of the power of the short 'sting' in being able to tag commercials where time is precious. In fact, the advertising world tends to view sonic logos as the single greatest opportunity in sonic branding. As a result, the overwhelming majority of Sonicbrand projects involve the creation of a sonic logo. It is an intellectually sound place to start the creation of sonic branding that will be heard by external audiences because it is simply the sonic equivalent of a visual mark and every brand in existence has a visual representation of itself.

Intel

What makes a great sonic logo? The best place to start answering that question must be with the examination of the most recognized and successful sonic logo to date. Today, Intel is one of the top ten brands in the world, according to Interbrand's annual study of brand value. This is a remarkable position for the brand to be in, when one considers what it does and where it has come from.

The personal computer (PC) market in the 1980s was driven by computer and software manufacturers. The badge on the box was of primary importance in consumer decision-making: Atari, Sinclair, Commodore, BBC, Apricot and Apple were the flavours of the time when IBM compatibility was still a special product feature and Windows was just a twinkle in Bill Gates' eye. Even if a consumer was not interested in the brand of hardware, their priority might be a word processor or a spreadsheet facility; they would buy a PC of indistinct manufacture for a single software function.

Interestingly, the major PC brands of the 1980s marketed their new products according to the amount of random access memory (RAM) that they packed. Thus, the Commodore 64 had 64 kilobytes of RAM. Similarly, Clive Sinclair's Spectrum's showed their progress through the years from the ZX81, with a whopping 1 k of RAM to the 16, 48 and 128 k machines. Very few people knew or cared about the speed of the microprocessor. Fewer still bothered to find out who made it but this all changed with the success of the IBM PC and the many clones that were sold in their wake. Things started to alter at the end of the 1980s and it was Intel that made the difference in how PCs were marketed and what is now deemed to be the most important feature of a PC.

Intel had always believed in the power of the processor. Gordon Moore, co-founder, was the man responsible for Moore's Law, which stated in 1964 that the number of transistors on a microprocessor would roughly double every 18 months. Together with Bob Noyce, the inventor of the integrated circuit, he founded Intel in 1968 and the business grew and grew through their manufacture of chips for everything from pocket calculators to traffic lights. The big success, however, was to come in 1981 when Intel won a contract to supply IBM with a chip for the first IBM PC. The success of that machine and the Intel-powered clones made Intel a very big and very rich company.

Strangely for such a successful business, however, Intel had virtually no brand awareness among consumers, who were still being fed on RAM and software applications. In 1989, Intel decided that it no longer wanted to be just another component and that it might benefit in the long run if consumers knew the operating speeds of chips and had an understanding that the chip was the core component of their new PC. Essentially, Intel decided to change the marketing agenda for PCs and they wanted to change it in their own favour.

Dennis Carter, an Intel marketing manager in 1989, is the man who has gone down in corporate history for creating Intel's consumer brand awareness. With his team, he set about informing information technology (IT) purchasers that it was the 386SX processor that was the key to the potential of their new PCs. The initiative was so successful that other chip manufacturers also started talking about their 386 processors. 386 was not a trademark, just a code number for the chip and it proved unprotectable. So, Intel needed a stronger, distinct and ownable brand name for its chips that would allow it to maintain its difference in the market.

Carter had a couple of interesting challenges to overcome. First, there was much scepticism as to whether anyone would really be interested in a microprocessor brand or whether Intel's team were up to the task. Second, Intel was only ever a component in other people's products, no consumers just bought a chip, so building the Intel brand would require the co-operation of PC manufacturers. History tells us that the sceptics were wrong and that the co-operative strategy employed would turn out to be the cornerstone of Intel's consumer communications.

After studying the marketing activity of existing 'ingredient' brands such as NutraSweet™, Teflon™ and Dolby™, Carter's ad agency Dahlin, Smith and White, came up with the advertising strap-line 'Intel. The computer inside'. The values they sought to communicate with their launch ads were 'safety', 'leading technology' and reliability. Happily for Intel and their agency, this first activity proved effective at building consumer awareness of Intel and building confidence in the brand.

With the shortening of the strap-line to 'Intel Inside', came a co-operative advertising programme that sought to communicate the benefits of Intel chips to every PC buyer in the world. Very simply, Intel offered to give a rebate to PC manufacturers of a percentage of the money the manufacturer spent on Intel chips. This rebate was for the sole purpose of co-funding press advertising which had to carry the Intel Inside logo with some strictly laid out specifications regarding its size and prominence.

The programme launched in 1991 and within six months had signed up 300 PC manufacturers. At the start of 1992, Intel launched its first brand TV commercials (made by Industrial Light and Magic). The success of the first campaigns meant that TV and radio became acceptable media for Intel's co-op ad budgets. As a result, by 1995 a need was identified for an audio visual version of the Intel Inside logo. Though it had become common in press ads and stickers on the front of PCs, in those places it was static. TV and radio gave the logo the chance to move and sound and Intel was not going to pass up the chance to use the media to their full potential.

The man responsible for the Intel sonic logo is Walter Werzowa. His company, which has a long heritage in advertising and film scoring, created the now famous sonic logo to accompany the movement of the animated visual logo and sought not just to make a mnemonic but to create a logo with emotional content, in the same way as a film score works. The Intel sonic logo starts with an atonal 'hit' of 20 different sounds, including a tambourine, an anvil, an electric spark and a hammer hitting a pipe. The following four notes (D flat, G flat, D flat, A flat) are played using a mix of marimba, xylophone, bells and a 'secret recipe' of instruments.

It is now thought that the Intel Inside sonic is heard every five minutes in an ad somewhere in the world, which is a testament to just how much Intel has invested in building its brand. The fact that it has been investing so consistently heavily in the same five-note property for seven years is the reason that Intel's sonic logo stands alone as the most recognized in the world. Because it was created to convey the emotions of the brand, not just to be memorable, it has stood the test of time.

The other important factor in its longevity is the strict guidelines that have been created for its usage. The 'signature ID audio-visual logo' as Intel call it, is always treated with reverence in ads. It is generally placed within the main body of an ad, rather than as an end device and it is given clear air around it – no other sounds are ever allowed to compete with it. As a result, the three seconds of logo has proved more memorable than the 60 seconds of PC manufacturer ad that surrounds it. The overall take-out from watching an Intel co-funded ad is that Intel endorses the PC manufacturer with its sign of quality and technological assurance.

As described earlier, the principles of successful branding, the creation of brand properties that are distinct, memorable, flexible and honest apply equally to the sonic logo. It is against these criteria, as well as the brand brief, audits and agreed sonic language that the sonic logo must be judged.

CHAPTER 22

Sonic guidelines

The third component of the sonic brand identity is the guidelines document. In conjunction with the brand score and the sonic logo, this document should contain all the strategic, technical and creative information required to create expressions of the brand that are consistent with the identity and thereby relate back to the belief and values of the brand. Guidelines documents can vary greatly, dependent upon the scope for sonic branding exposed during the audit phase. Each sonic touchpoint will require its own guidelines and as a result, the document can become very weighty indeed.

Creatively, the guidelines should describe the sonic language, brand score and sonic logo adequately that two skilled composers could create new works that fit seamlessly with one another and have the desired emotional fit with the brand. The compositional guidelines, therefore, must include musically technical information such as the melodic and harmonic structure of the brand score and sonic logo. Standard musical notation is used to describe this.

Melody

Melody is defined as the series, one after another, of musical notes that make up a tune. Melody is the component of music that is most readily processed by our brains, requiring a low level of involvement from the listener to become recognizable and memorable. It is generally the melody of a piece of music that we will whistle after listening. It is rare, except for the most involved and trained musician, to remember and whistle a bass line or rhythm guitar part of a popular song.

Because of the ease and speed with which we remember melodies, this part of the identity is usually at the very heart of the sonic logo and always forms a major part of the brand score and guidelines.

Harmony

If melody is the series of notes, defining harmony is to identify the notes that are placed in parallel, underneath the melody. Sonic guidelines are not always the place for advanced musical theory but some reference to the type of harmonies that are core to the identity is generally deemed useful. In this way, specific modes of harmony as might be archetypal of jazz or rock or classic styles can be defined for future reference.

Key signature

The key is a particularly important piece of information for establishing a creative platform that can be built upon independently by composers. The key of a piece of music describes which set of related notes have been used and the notes that can seamlessly be used in further work.

Simplistically, there are two types of key: major and minor. Major keys sound characteristically comfortable and minor keys are characteristically interesting.

Time signature

One other element of the compositional guidelines that is always included is the time signature, which defines the overall rhythmic feel of the brand score. Thus, by defining a key and a rhythm in the guidelines, we can help ensure that all subsequent sonic branding has a basis in the identity.

A full description of the sonic language is also desirable. This is the technical definition of the instruments used, including, where applicable, the names of keyboards, sound modules or samplers and the settings employed. Again, this is very useful information for composers and ensures consistency in all new work.

On some occasions, for example where singing has been used as a part of the language, the contact details of an individual performer have been included in guidelines as they have provided a unique contribution to the sonic language. A specific vocal element may or may not become a key brand property but should it do so, it is important that future sonic branding can utilize the same voice and thus be consistent.

For some brands, voice is incredibly important and guidelines are required for generating consistency in spoken language. Tone of voice guidelines have become a speciality of Engine, a London-based ideation company, whose work has included the development of detailed vocal guidelines for the global mobile brand, Orange. Below, Oliver King, a director of Engine, describes the work in his own words.

'Hello, it's me!'

For many businesses the use of a voice to represent their brand is limited to voiceovers in advertising campaigns. Some choose these voices extremely well; and they become synonymous with the products or services they provide, for example James Earl Jones with CNN or Jeff Goldblum with Apple. But for other businesses, especially those who are predominately experienced by customers through voice-based services, their choice of voice is even more important. For them it represents a primary medium through which to build and express their brand.

Orange, probably the world's most coveted telecommunications brand, have long understood the benefits a voice can bring to their business. So when they were exploring 'brand' issues surrounding voices, they asked Engine, a London-based ideation consultancy, to work with them to develop some guidelines that they could use to ensure that the voices they selected were 'on-brand' and exhibited the right qualities for the services they were intended. With Orange's permission, these are some of the ideas we developed and used together.

Why bother?

The first thing that needed to be understood was why guidelines on voices were needed at all? As a telecommunications brand voices are an integral part of Orange's business, but as the business grew, and more voices were commissioned without a common point of reference, there were concerns that some were more appropriate than others. The problem that the brand marketeers at Orange faced was that there was very little information available in the public domain that helped them justify and explain why good, considered voices were important. So, in order to develop a case for the project, a few obvious and not so obvious points needed to be made.

Consistency

Brands have long understood the importance of consistency in building relationships with customers. And just as it's important to have consistent messages, behaviour and look-and-feel, it's equally important to sound consistent as well. With a business the size of Orange with voice-services and advertising campaigns in a dozen different languages, defining what they sound like is as important as defining what they look like.

Recognition

For many brands their look-and-feel has been refined so much over the years that you can distinguish them visually without even seeing a logo. This has the advantage of raising the awareness of your brand with customers without them having to concentrate too hard to see it. But if you're dealing with an audio environment you really have to listen hard to what's being said to understand who's behind it; often you actually need to hear the name of the company – the equivalent of seeing a logo. If the voices you use with your brand were recognizable, you wouldn't need to rely on customers actively listening to become aware of your brand. So just as a strong visual identity helps customers to spot you, a strong audio identity will help them hear you as well.

Credibility

Sounding credible is very important. In the real world we're highly attuned to picking out things that don't sound quite right, or making judgements about the quality or reliability of the information we hear, based on the sound of the voice that delivers it. For a voice-service to be effective it needs to sound as if it knows what it's talking about. If a voice doesn't sound 'right', human nature will ensure that what's heard will be treated with a degree of scepticism. We'll suggest a technique for establishing credibility later.

Subjectivity

Selecting a voice can be a hard decision to take – although it needn't be! For most people who commission voices, the decision is simply taken on whether or not they like the voice. This can be OK if you're choosing a voice for an advertising campaign because you have a degree of artistic licence that can be refined with the next campaign if it doesn't quite work. But if you're choosing one for a voice-service – a service you intend to spend millions on developing – it's a little bit more important.

Table 22.1	The four types of voice-service	
Type	Description	Interaction level
1. Call Management	Designed to help customers navigate through call centres. These services offer pre-recorded prompts to push button selections made by customers.	Low
2. Automated Tele-Sale	Designed to help customers purchase things like tickets. These systems either work around the prompt and push button system or are programmed to listen out for a very specific response from the caller – 'if you would like sales, say "yes" now'.	medium
3. Interactive Voice Response	Designed to provide customer services and operate similarly to the tele-sales systems. An example of one of these would be interactive voice mail, where users can listen, respond to and save voice messages.	high
4. Intelligent Voice Recognition	State of the art systems that actually listen to what people say and reply intelligently. In the future you'll be able to ask natural questions or give natural commands within the service and it will respond accordingly. These systems are increasingly based on entirely virtual text-to-speech applications with limited pre-recorded prompts.	high

As Table 22.1 shows, customers physically interact with voice-services – they have an experience. And the way a voice sounds can have a real effect on your experience, which can make the difference between the service being accepted, celebrated and earning money – and it not.

Choosing a voice for a voice-service has a perceived risk attached: companies will spend a lot of time and money recording or programming the voice they choose, which can be extremely hard to change later. So getting it right from the start is a must. Decisions of this scale need to be based on sound rationales and objective analysis, not just personal tastes.

Choosing a voice

From the start Orange wanted to ensure that any voices they choose were unique, different and recognizably theirs. To do this they first had to understand what the market sounded like.

Audio audit

Orange began by reviewing a broad spectrum of voice-services that their customers might encounter. This included the voices they used, those their competitors used and voice-services their customers might encounter in their daily lives. As a result, two things became apparent: most of the voices sounded the same (young, white, middle-class females with Received Pronunciation – think of it as 1980s BBC English). And, if you listened beyond the scripts they were reading, to the qualities of the voice and the way the words were spoken, they almost all suggested different values to the values of the brands they represented.

Try this...

Make a list of a variety of voice-services you've heard from other brands, write down the values you'd expect these brands to portray, then listen to the theme and note down the values you actually hear in the voice. Are they the same?

To Orange the results of the audit showed that developing distinct voices would be valuable because all the existing voices were so similar; and that nobody else appeared to be using 'branded' voices, which meant their hunch for learning how to develop them was entirely appropriate.

Deconstructing a voice

To understand how to 'brand' a voice, Orange first of all had to take one apart. The process began by recognizing and exploring two insights from common experience. The first is that people often make split-second decisions about what they think someone is like, just based on what they sound like, what they wear and how they behave. The second is that when you listen to someone's voice over the phone for the first time, when you don't

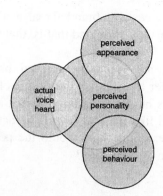

Figure 22.1 Hypothetical model linking voice to listener's perception

know what they look like, you start to construct an imaginary personality and appearance for that person in your mind.

These insights enabled Orange to establish a hypothetical model that linked the sound of a voice to the listener's perception of what a real person behind that voice might be like. This meant that a voice couldn't be treated in isolation to the perceived personality it suggests.

Recognizing that voices carry encoded clues that listeners use to build and judge imaginary personalities by, it was clear that the personality they should imagine should be the brand.

Personality

Orange defined two levels to the personality that they wanted to get their listeners to perceive. One was the brand's personality and the other was the personality of a real-world character: someone who would be good at providing the services the voice-service provides but in the real world. For example, if you're providing banking services perhaps you should try to portray the personality of a really good bank cashier?

Composite personality

Brand personality   +   *real-world*   =   *composite personality of*
(brand values)   *personality*   *the voice-service*

Developing voice-services with branded real-world personalities helps to give credibility to the service. Provided that is, that the service isn't at odds with your brand.

Personality profiles are typically defined on the OCEAN model (see Table 22.2). In order to establish the profiles for the real-world characters, Orange used this model to explore, define and evaluate the sort of personalities that they'd like the real-world characters to have. For example, to take an earlier example, how would the personality of an Orange bank cashier differ from an AOL one?

Vocal qualities

Having established the personality a voice should portray Orange then needed to understand how it should actually sound. When you listen to a voice, the message you receive depends on a couple of things: the language used, and the way it's spoken.

Language – literally in terms of native tongue or accent, and vocabulary – can be defined easily. If you want a Spanish voice reading a script in French, you can have it. What's hardest is describing what the vocal qualities of that voice should be.

Table 22.2   OCEAN personality profile model
A personality profile is established by asking the subject a series of semantic questions and scoring their responses. Their profile can then be charted across the five personality dimensions shown below.

openness	*High scorers tend to be original, creative, curious, complex; low scorers tend to be conventional, down to earth, have narrow interests and not be very creative.*
conscientiousness	*High scorers tend to be reliable, well-organized, self-disciplined, careful; low scorers tend to be disorganized, undependable, negligent.*
extroversion	*High scorers tend to be sociable, friendly, fun-loving, talkative; low scorers tend to be introverted, reserved, inhibited, quiet.*
agreeableness	*High scorers tend to be good-natured, sympathetic, forgiving, courteous; low scorers tend to be critical, rude, harsh, even callous!*
neuroticism	*High scorers tend to be nervous, highly strung, insecure, worrying; low scorers tend to be calm, relaxed, secure.*

Table 22.3	Typical adjectives used to describe voices in the UK			
baby	effeminate	hollow	silken	rough
bell-like	forced	heavy	low	whining
bubbly	heady	nasal	ringing	sultry
clangy	dark	light	timid	mature
brilliant	golden	open	silvery	throaty
black	high	hoarse	masculine	wet
chesty	feminine	pinched	sharp	whiskey
cutting	flat	shallow	white	rough
constricted	gravelly	resonant	stentorian	pushed
burnished	metallic	pingy	strident	husky
deep	immature	thin	velvety	harsh

Descriptive adjectives

To understand vocal qualities, Orange began by exploring adjectives that were used to describe voices in the UK. It soon became clear that they were quite subjective and tended to describe a voice as a whole. The adjectives were also idiomatic – they didn't translate well between different languages. So interpreting responses to a voice using descriptions like these was not precise enough, or culturally consistent. For example, in the UK 'shallow' might be used to describe a voice that was quite quiet, without a great range in pitch; in Thailand, however, it might be translated to mean not very deep.

Vocal attributes

As a global brand Orange realized that to maintain any form of consistency they needed to describe a voice as a fundamental set of vocal attributes that could be transferable between different cultures. With a little research and a lot of listening they developed a set of 14 attributes that they could use to describe the sound of a voice.

These attributes provided development teams with a common language that could be used to brief and critique a voice. This was especially important when you consider that those responsible for briefing, selecting and evaluating a voice probably have no formal training in the subject, so this list enabled them to explain what they liked or didn't like in a performance to voice artists, voiceover agencies and voice coaches.

Table 22.4	The 14 vocal attributes
Rhythm	the way emphasis is placed on what's said
Pitch	high to low
Melody	the way rhythm and pitch is combined
Pace	the speed of delivery
Musical tone	the overall musical quality of the voice
Intonation	the way what's said is related to how it's said
Energy	through expressing engagement with the content
Clarity	of delivery
Muscular tension	muscular tension governing the sound of the voice
Resonance	the place of vibration for the voice (nose, throat, chest)
Pause	using pauses to add meaning between the words
Breath	how and when you breathe
Commitment	communicating belief in what's said
Volume	the amount of sound produced

Describing a voice

By using these attributes, Orange were able to explain what they meant when they described a voice as, for example, 'dynamic'.

A dynamic voice has a stimulating rhythm, its pace is motivated and its pitch is adaptive. Its tone is true and its intonation supports the meaning of what's being said. It's full of energy, has an elevated volume. It's clear, relaxed, has full resonance. Pauses are used to add meaning, and its breathing is centred. It has an engaging melody and it is assertive.

These descriptions are most powerful when you contrast them. Look at Table 22.5 which compares a dynamic voice to a steadfast one.

By considering the values of their brand against the attributes Orange were able to describe, in terms that were easily understood, what their values should sound like.

The descriptions in Table 22.5 are for a British voice. Naturally if the voice were French, Thai or Hebrew the descriptions attached to each attribute would change.

Combining brand values and personality

Armed with the real-world personality profile, and the description of an Orange voice, finding the right voice for a new service is straightforward. See Table 22.6.

Table 22.5   Contrasting two voices

a 'dynamic' voice		a 'steadfast' voice
stimulating	**Rhythm**	syncopated
motivated	**Pace**	measured
adaptive	**Pitch**	controlled
true	**Tone**	balanced
supportive	**Intonation**	precise
elevated	**Volume**	constant
full	**Energy**	full
clear	**Clarity**	clear
relaxed	**Tension**	relaxed
full	**Resonance**	full
meaningful	**Pause**	deliberate
centred	**Breath**	even
engaging	**Melody**	plodding
assertive	**Commitment**	consistent

Table 22.6   Finding the right voice

Step 1	Conduct a workshop to define the real-world personality of the character behind the voice-service. Use the OCEAN model.
Step 2	Using the attributes, write a description of how your brand would sound in a voice.
Step 3	Use the personality profile and voice description as part of a brief to a voice agency and ask them to provide a broad selection of voices that they think match.
Step 4	With the workshop team review the voices against the voice descriptions and dismiss any that are off-brand. With the remainder, do a perceived personality test by marking each voice against the OCEAN model again.
Step 5	The voice that is closest to the real-world personality profile is the one you should use.

A voice is a complex thing and it can be an extremely powerful tool in helping you to build and express your brand. If you do it well, like Orange, the voices you choose will match pre-determined personality profiles and carry encoded qualities that whisper the values of your brand in your customers ears.

If a brand is anything, it's the intangible aspect of your company that your competitors can't copy and that your customers form relationships with. Developing voice-services with endearing personalities that are recognizably yours can only help to attract and retain customers for longer, thereby earning your business more money. Furthermore, if the individual voice-service characters you develop are distinct, it will make it easier for you to develop a distinctive family of service characters each credible and engaging in its own way, and each expressing the values of your brand.

What would we say to wrap this up? Ensure the voices you use sound credible, make sure they: have endearing personalities; don't reinforce stereotypes; are memorable; and are different. The future's bright, the future's Orange.

CHAPTER 23

Sonic logo

Particular reference within the guidelines must be given to how and where to use the sonic logo. The visual symbols of brands are important, often viewed with a reverence that dictates they should be used sparingly and sympathetically. The guidelines for a sonic logo must convey the same understanding.

It is always going to be undesirable to overplay a logo, just as it is undesirable to neglect it and not play it enough to gain recognition and build associations. The guidelines, therefore, must lay out the rules for when and where the sonic logo is to be employed, as well as identifying the key applications where the sonic logo could have particular resonance.

A checklist for usage of a sonic logo on television is shown in Table 23.1. The same questions and evaluations need to be made for commercial radio; Table 23.2 indicates additional points to consider here.

An area of specific interest with regard to radio, rather than TV communications is opportunities to hear (OTH). Radio tends to deliver more frequency of exposure than television, because of its relatively low media costs, so the danger of creating listener fatigue to a single sonic logo is far greater. Listener fatigue is the single greatest hazard in the usage of a sonic logo. Very high frequency of exposure will tend, in many instances, to lessen the effectiveness of any sound to draw attention. Furthermore, the ability of a sonic logo to cause audiences to switch from hearing the radio to listening directly to a brand communication will usually be diminished with overplaying.

Sonic logos will behave like any sound that is heard so often that it becomes wallpaper. Think of the person who lives next to the railway but sleeps through the night no matter how trains pass. The brain can become accustomed to sounds and learn to ignore them. Thus, the overall frequency or OTH of any sonic logo must be carefully monitored.

There is no universal truth, however, regarding effective frequency. The optimum number of exposures is not yet known but there is a common-sense correlation between the musical complexity of a logo and the OTH at

Table 23.1   Usage guidelines for TV

TV	
Brand ads	Call to action or end-frame device?
	Volume relative to soundtrack?
	Underscore for voiceover?
	Voice around not over?
Tactical ads	As above, plus
	Is there time?
	Does the message support the brand?
	Is the logo appropriate for the context?
Co-branded or	Timing?
ingredient ads	Clear air around logo?
(Intel strategy)	Volume and positioning
	relative to co-brand's logo?
Programme sponsorships	How many idents per show/per week?
	Is there room for the logo in all idents?
	What is the desired frequency of logo exposure?
	Is a new version required to fit programming
	context? (Desired)

Table 23.2   Usage guidelines for commercial radio

Radio – as TV plus:	
Promotions	Call to action or end device?
	Volume relative to the rest
	of the ad?
	Underscore for voice over?
	Voice around not over?

which listener fatigue will become an issue. The relationship is as follows: a sonic logo made up solely of a simple melody line, played on one instrument, will be very easily remembered and understood. In Europe, an example of such a sonic is the one that belongs to Direct Line, the insurance services group.

Direct Line

If you have heard it once, it is as if you have heard it a 1,000 times. It holds no mystery or complexity. It is a fairly generic 'cavalry charge', played with heavily synthesized brass sounds. It was created under the aegis of ad agency Davis Wilkins around 1989 in the UK, when Direct Line launched as one of the first telephone-based companies in Europe. Chris Wilkins, creative director of the agency at the time is said to have described the sonic logo as an 'old fashioned advertising gimmick'. It is said by Andrew Ingram, now of the Radio Advertising Bureau (RAB) but then account planner at Davis Wilkins, that the development of a sonic logo, together with a visual counterpart, a red telephone on wheels, was encouraged by Steve Ashman, marketing manager at Direct Line, because he believed they would maximize results from audience testing of memorability, branding, communication strength and persuasive power.

In the tests, specifically the Link™ test carried out by research company Millward Brown, Ashman was proved correct. Direct Line's launch TV commercial is said to have 'blown the numbers off the dial'. The sight of the little red telephone driving over a hill to the rescue, accompanied by the sound of a cavalry charge played on what sounded like a telephone keypad had tremendous resonance. The launch activity ran for around six months on television and by the time follow-up activity was being planned, the red phone and the sonic logo had become a part of the TV audience's understanding of the brand to such an extent that it was deemed impossible to drop the sonic from future advertising.

Direct Line was and remains one of the most important launches ever in the UK insurance market and it set an agenda for 'direct' marketing of services from the supplier to the consumer via the telephone that continues to impact countless brands in the UK. Almost every retail sector now has a number of players with 'direct' in their brand name as a consequence of Direct Line's impact as a business model and as a consumer launch.

The ad campaign won the Institute of Practitioners in Advertising (IPA) award for effectiveness in both generating response and building a brand at the same time. At the start of the 1990s, this was one of the holy grails of the media planning and buying industry and Direct Line became an iconic brand for those working in the industry just as it had for audiences. Creatively, too, Direct Line was aspirational to such an extent that a number of copycats hit the insurance market very quickly. Most notable of these was Admiral Insurance. It launched in 1993 with a strategy closely mirroring that of Direct Line. It had an admiral, holding a telescope to his eye, on the lookout for the best insurance quotes and he had his own sonic logo to accompany his search. Like Direct Line, the sonic logo was a single melody line, this time a sailor's hornpipe rather than a cavalry charge. It was played on a synthesized instrument of no discernable lineage but it sounded very, very similar to the synthesized brass of the Direct Line logo.

The similarities were so close that in research carried out by the sonics team at Capital Radio, there was over 70% misattribution of the Admiral sonic back to Direct Line.

It was pretty clear that the copycat sound was potentially damaging to both brands and Admiral seems to have abandoned it some time in 1998. Admiral, though, made Direct Line realize that its sonic logo was too open to being copied by other brands and, in 1998, they made some changes. The melody of its logo become more distinct – replacing the traditional, generic cavalry charge – and was made longer. The arrangement became slightly more complex, too. This allowed the new logo to become easily copyrightable as a piece of music, as a result of which it became easier for Direct Line to apply for and gain trademark status for its sonic logo.

The Direct Line logo is incredibly powerful and is well respected within the organization for what it does. Jim Wallace, marketing director of the insurance company, who oversaw its regeneration and trademark registration, told us that the audio-visual logo regularly achieves astonishing results in research groups. Recognition and recall levels of over 90% are the norm, the kind of levels that only Coca-Cola and other 'top' brands usually achieve.

Sonicbrand's own research tells us that people in the UK do remember the Direct Line sonic logo more than any other apart from Intel. This has a potential downside to it, however, in that the same research shows Direct Line's sonic logo to be the most irritating around. This is not necessarily the bad news it seems. First it is only irritating because it is so memorable. Second, the 'irritating' sound of the logo ensures that it cuts through the background hum of advertising and grabs attention; it is most definitely distinct in the current marketplace. Third, the simplicity of the logo fits emotionally with the simplicity of the offering.

Direct Line has recognized that their logo is potentially irritating and altered the way they use it to accommodate this factor. It is not overplayed. It is not on every ad for every product and it is sometimes used quite softly as underscore to a voiceover and only rarely given a full volume, 'listen to me' outing. Wallace makes the excellent point that the redesign of the logo has created a musical property that could, if the need arose, be extended into full brand scores, which would give the brand some healthy flexibility in its approach to future sonic branding.

On your marks

Sound trademarks have been in practical use since African villages started identifying themselves through distinct drumming patterns a few thousand years ago. In legal terms, however, the first sound mark registered was in 1950, in the US. In that year, the National Broadcasting Company (NBC), applied to the US Patent and Trademark Office (USPTO) for a registered sound mark for radio broadcast services. The application was successful and US Reg. No. 0523616 was granted.

The mark related to what were already the famous NBC chimes, which had first been broadcast on 29 November 1929. On that first and every subsequent day, the notes were struck at 59 minutes 30 seconds, and 29 minutes 30 seconds past the hour and served to help co-ordinate the output of NBC's many affiliated radio stations scattered around the US. The mark subsequently expired 1971 and NBC reapplied and was granted US Reg. No. 0916552 for '3 chime like notes' to identify broadcasting services. The mark is now most frequently used between television shows to identify the station. Among older audiences it is thought to be the most recognizable sound mark in the US.

Another famous US sound mark belongs to AOL Time Warner. The theme to the *Merrie Melodies* was registered in July 2001 (US Reg. No. 2,473,248). This is the full piece of musical score that has been used as the soundtrack for the *Looney Toons* cartoon series since the early 1930s. It was originally a loose musical arrangement of the classic rhyme 'Merrily We Roll Along', by Charles Tobias, Murray Mencher and Eddie Cantor. Through many decades of association, however, it has become inextricably linked with Tweety Pie, Sylvester and particularly Bugs Bunny saying the immortal words 'That's All Folks'. The tune and arrangement, of course, have always been protected by copyright but as time passes and the composers unfortunately die, copyright ceases to protect the tune for AOL. Musical copyright runs out 70 years after the death of the composer and only now that the tune is a trademark, will there be some perpetual protection in law for AOL Time Warner.

Perhaps the most famous test-case for sound marks was brought by Harley-Davidson, the motorcycle manufacturers and lifestyle brand. In the mid-1990s, it filed for trademark status for the aural emissions of its 45 degree V-twin single crankpin motor. Though the Patent Office granted the mark, it was still subject to objections and delays from other motorcycle manufacturers some six years after its application in 1994. As a result, Harley decided to abandon the case. Joanne Bischmann, a vice president of marketing, stated at the time: 'If our customers know the sound cannot be imitated, that's good enough for Harley-Davidson'.[1]

One of the more bizarre sound marks successfully registered in the US is for 'the sound of the famous Tarzan yell' US Reg. No. 2,210,506. It was applied for and won by Edgar Rice Burroughs Inc. and is described in the registry as the 'famous Tarzan yell' followed by the exact name of the notes and pitches comprising the mark.

The strangest mark, however, must be the one applied for by the Minnesota State Lottery, in the United States. It has filed the following application (US S/N 76/077221) to register its sound mark for lottery services: 'The mark is the sound of a wild loon provided in one or more short bursts, either alone or with background music at the end of an oral presentation on radio or television advertising the lottery services.' So, wild loons in the US could be trademarks but in other parts of the world, there are equally interesting sound marks. In New Zealand, for example, Unilever, the UK-based FMCG conglomerate, has registered the sound of the friction between finger or thumb and a plate that has been cleaned with a Unilever-brand washing-up liquid. The trademark is nothing more or less than a 'squeak' but nonetheless New Zealand Reg. No. 247094 was granted.

Most major markets allow for sound marks and there are some that have been registered in multiple territories. For example, Deutsche Telekom AG of Germany has registered its 'five note musical score' in the United States (Reg. No. 2,459,405), New Zealand (Reg. No. 649629) and Germany, which gives it full EU registration. The 'five-tone' Intel Corporation sound is registered in the United States, Australia and New Zealand but interestingly, not in Europe.

European Union trademark law allows for sound marks and the process for registering a sound mark in Europe is similar to that for a visual mark in most respects but takes a little while longer. How much longer, depends upon how serious you are about registration. Sound marks are applied for via the trademark registry in the same way as visual marks. An application is made if it is thought likely that there will be no infringement upon existing sound marks, it is then published by the registry. In an obvious difference to the visual process, the application will include the written description and musical notation for the mark, if applicable, rather than a drawing. The melody or sound will ideally be original and distinct. It is possible that a melody that is in the public domain could become a sound mark but it is much harder to make a successful application if the logo is not copyright the applicant.

A burden is placed upon the applicant to prove that the sound mark that is being applied for already has a resonance with the audience for that brand. This is different to the visual process, where a trademark may well be new and possibly not yet even seen or heard of by an audience. That a sonic logo has built recognition and become linked to a brand must be proved through research. If it is, then it is very likely the sound mark application will be successful. Direct Line gained the necessary associations in under six months. This has as much to do with their weight of advertising as it has to do with the distinctiveness of their logo. Had they advertised less, it is entirely possible that it could have taken many years to build sufficient recognition in their logo to make its sound mark registration straightforward. The registry is in the public domain for a period of six months, during which time challenges to the application can be made. Should no challenge arise, registration itself takes around one more year.

The benefits of a sonic logo being registerable as a sound mark are considerable. Not least of them is the protection afforded by the legal concept of 'passing off'. Should a competitor like your sonic logo so much that they get their own and it sounds a lot like yours, where similarities or high levels of misattribution can be proved then it is fairly straightforward to enforce a 'cease and desist' upon the new entrant.

CHAPTER 24

Technical considerations

The next section of the guidelines relates primarily to the playback of the sonic logo, which at this stage is the only sonic branding element for external use. It is important that the logo is heard at every touchpoint as it was designed to be heard. The broad range of media and applications make the management of playback a challenge, particularly in relation to the audio quality of playback equipment.

Any set of speakers will have their own characteristics that have a direct impact upon the sounds that are heard; specifically the upper and lower frequency limits are of interest as these dictate the highest and lowest tones that can be played. Laptop computer speakers, such as those on an Apple Powerbook, are very small and have a relatively high lower frequency limit. As a result, very low bass sounds will not be heard at all through them and percussive bass sounds often come out as clicks rather than booms.

In our work for Element 6, where a key use for the sonic logo was as a part of a laptop presentation, this was important to know during the creative process and important for the guidelines for future work. If melody had been played by a bass instrument, which would have sounded perfectly good in the studio, as soon as it was played in context it would have been lost to the small range of the speakers. When creating a sonic logo for Shazam Entertainment, the main channel for which was the mobile phone, the frequency limits of mobile earpieces was a key factor in the composition of the sonic logo and the knowledge gained in the creative process proved a valuable resource for the guidelines.

Speaker technology has improved rapidly in the last ten years, with smaller speakers now delivering a greater frequency range with greater clarity. Much of this is to do with digital technology and it is all good news for sonic branding. Every new set of speakers represents a new sonic touchpoint for the brand. Personal digital assistants (PDAs) in particular, are proliferating and the inclusion of speakers within them means that many people are now walking around with devices capable of delivering sonically branded messages. Most speakers, even laptop computer speakers, are capable of reasonable-quality playback of the higher frequencies of sound, which rely less upon the size of the speaker. Thus, with guidelines in place, it is possible to create very meaningful versions of sonic logos for small speaker applications, while full-frequency versions are used for media such as TV or radio, where speakers are generally larger and able to deal with lower frequencies.

When Web applications play a part in the sonic branding, thought has to be given in the guidelines as to the compression rates of digital files and the size of file that can be accommodated within the website without hindering download times. In the creation of guidelines for the RAB, the Web was a major application and thus the nature of the file (in this case an MP3 was preferred) together with the recommended playback platform (Flash) had to be included in the guidelines.

Sonic logos are rarely used in an environmental setting but when they are, or where in-store or office environments will ultimately be an important touchpoint for the sonic branding, the configuration and specification of speaker systems can become an important topic for the guidelines. In these cases, sonic branding guidelines will focus upon creative and strategic aims, while specialist acousticians, who bring their scientific knowledge of sound to bear on this very complex subject, will be employed to draft acoustic guidelines.

Among many other potentially relevant pieces of information for the technical guidelines are bit depth, sample rates and relative levels for the mix of future sonic branding. Additionally, it may be relevant to have mastering specifications laid out by medium so as to ensure a consistent sound for all sonic branding. Mastering is an important finishing process in the creation of music. It can be viewed in a similar way to the application of fixative to a pastel drawing. It creates 'oneness' in the music but to have the right effect across different media will usually require slightly different mastering for each version. For example, an FM radio version of the logo would be mastered differently to a laptop version.

CHAPTER 25

Experience

Stage one to three of the sonic branding engine are fundamentally concerned with how a brand seeks to identify itself in sound. These stages lead to the creation of a model and a set of internal management tools that can be referenced by all those who seek to represent a brand to its stakeholders; ad agencies, interactive designers, call centre managers and so on. It is important for all those in control of a brand touchpoint to take responsibility for the relationship they establish with the stakeholders and to ensure it is consistent with the brand and its values. It is crucial to this relationship that a sonic identity is referenced and for the framework it provides to be appreciated if a brand experience is to be effective. To make an analogy with visual branding, stages one to three create the typographic style, a logo and a framework in which these can be utilized. Stage four turns these visual elements into letterheads, uniforms and signage that all communicate something about the brand.

The keys to ensuring that the sonic identity is effective wherever a brand seeks to communicate with its stakeholders are the branding criteria of flexibility and consistency. The first three stages of the sonic branding engine provide points of distinctiveness and memorability by creating an understanding of the sounds that effectively communicate a brand and in doing so provide a palette of music, voice and ambient sounds with almost infinite flexibility. It is then up to those in charge of the various touchpoints to implement this palette in the most contextually sympathetic way. By opening up the world of sound to those who seek to communicate a brand it is possible to provide them with the creative tools they need to reach stakeholders in the best manner. Their understanding of their touchpoints and their audience makes them the right people to decide how the brand's sonic identity should be implemented and by providing a sonic palette and guidelines, it is possible to encourage creativity while being in a position to enforce consistency.

For too long now the controllers of the traditional media have feared sonic branding due to the constraints they feel it places on their creativity.

In fact sonic branding as explained in this book could be the key to unlocking creativity and allowing brands to take their stakeholders to places that they have never been. If a voice can communicate everything about a brand then there is the opportunity to take the visual elements to uncharted territories. If a sonic logo is as recognized as a visual one then there is no need for a pack-shot.

Brand experience, with the help of new technology, is changing and changing fast. Stakeholders are now able to exercise far greater control over the messages they receive and experiences they have. No longer is our understanding of a brand solely determined by a celebrity endorsement or an expensive advertisement during half-time at the Super Bowl. Brands must now understand every point at which they communicate with their stakeholders and must appreciate every context. They must learn to fit into people's lives seamlessly while at the same time encouraging them to take certain paths.

If brands are to retain their position in society they must learn to appreciate the true nature of experiences they can offer. They must learn to harness the power of each sense in order to remain distinct and relevant. They must understand the role they play in stakeholders' lives and ensure that they fulfil this role. They must quickly learn the potential for new technology and ensure they utilize it correctly and effectively. It would be too complicated to explore this role and how sound fits into it in all the experiences a brand can offer. Instead by providing an understanding of the scope of opportunities offered by sound we hope to allow brand-owners and communicators to fully explore its potential. The challenge is great and if brands are to be up to it they need to understand and appreciate what sound can do for them, then they must use it creatively.

Summary

There are more books to write. In this, to my knowledge the first and only book dedicated to the subject, we have examined the provenance of our subject and identified the core issues but we have only laid the foundations for a full understanding. Sonic branding, as you have read, is a large and amorphous subject that is evolving all the time and it is my hope that in committing the understanding that Sonicbrand has gathered to paper, that the evolution will be accelerated.

I spend far too much of my time listening to and being disappointed by how brands communicate with their stakeholders through sound and I want things to be different because sound, and music in particular, are very important, not just to me but to every one of us. I will let Aristotle have the final word:

> Music directly imitates the passions or states of the soul – gentleness, anger, courage, temperance and their opposites and other qualities; hence, when one listens to music that imitates a certain passion, one becomes imbued with the same passion; and if over a long period of time one habitually listens to the kind of music that rouses ignoble passions ones whole character will be shaped to an ignoble form. In short, if one listens to the wrong kind of music one will become the wrong kind of person; but conversely, if one listens to the right kind of music, one will tend to become the right kind of person.[1]

Appendix: dialogues

Jon Turner, executive creative director, Enterprise IG

Interview with Paul Fulberg and Dan Jackson, joint managing directors, Sonic brand. September 2002, Enterprise IG, Covent Garden, London WC2.

DJ   What is the difference between corporate identity (CI) and brand?

JT   CI was the industry up until a couple of years ago when it was based just upon the design of graphics to help a company look differently to its competitors.

    CI evolved to become branding. Branding, though, is not just CI with bells on; it is a new discipline that goes beyond graphic devices. Competitive companies need to express themselves in as many ways as they possibly can and branding is the process by which they do this.

DJ   A CI brief would appear to be fairly straightforward in terms of colours, shapes and fonts. Where does a brand brief start?

JT   Brand briefs can start in many different ways. Sometimes we are given an idea and asked to create the brand from its name down. More often, because of the budgets required to work with an agency like Enterprise IG, we will see a brand when it needs management leading towards a rebrand or a refresh.

    We do a lot of work with Ericcson, on the corporate side. There you have a company with a great heritage of brand that identified very early, by listening to its clients, that its brand could be in decline. The work we did was to help them, through a series of interviews and workshops and story-telling to rediscover the central belief of the business. For Ericcson, this was a great move. Where CI would have meant a new look and feel that might have plastered over underlying issues, the brand approach allowed us to uncover what the brand really means today.

    An example of the learning was a story relating to the actions of a senior personal assistant who, on hearing of an earthquake in a foreign country, on her own initiative sent crates of mobile phones to help the aid-workers. She was empowered to do this because she shared the beliefs of senior management that this would be the right thing to do. The branding exercise we did allowed her to share this story and lead to all the staff knowing that initiative would be applauded. This kind of story is a much more powerful communicator than graphic devices. When we get the chance to start with an internal audience, the branding process is incredibly rewarding.

DJ   You talk about brand story-telling and workshops. Do you think there is any point any more to brand values that expressed simply as words rather than through more expressive, collaborative processes?

JT   The problem is not with the idea of brand values but with the fact that some companies have been lazy with them. It is infuriating to find that a company has defined values that fail to differentiate it from the competition.

       Brand values, though, are still paramount. They form a backbone to the company's beliefs but they need to be researched well and that is where ideas like corporate story-telling are really useful.

DJ   Words alone can be misinterpreted. Is there an argument that one needs the more sophisticated communication of a story or perhaps some music, to really convey the emotions of a brand?

JT   I have never thought that words were enough. This is why we have developed living moodboards instead that use video, incorporating pictures, animations and music. We find living moodboards to be far more effective at getting our ideas across.

DJ   Music videos start with music and then fit the images. Feature films generally work the other way around. Which do you approach first the sound or the pictures?

JT   Sound is a crucial part of the moodboard but we are visual designers first and foremost. I do not think we are as au fait with music as we are with visuals. We don't have the skills to create, cut and paste it as we do with pictures. I'd be interested to start with music but we never have done.

PF   Since the logo came under attack from Naomi Klein and others, do you think branding is moving away from reliance upon the powerful corporate identity?

JT   Absolutely, but this was happening long before *No Logo* came out. I used to be the creative director of Bodyshop and Anita [Roddick] was always challenging how we saw the brand. As a franchise we tried to introduce many different coloured logos and we encouraged local franchisees to adapt the Bodyshop format to its geographical environment. For example, in Italy, all Bodyshops have marble floors.

       We also encouraged the use of local art in Bodyshops, with some incredibly powerful results, particularly in places like Northern Ireland. The global/local design ethos does need to be managed, though, or it can end up with bits of sellotape and kids drawings all over the place.

PF   McDonald's do the same thing. The branch outside Elland Road, the Leeds United ground allegedly has no red colours because of the Leeds United/Manchester United animosity.

JT   I love the way little stories like this come out of big corporations.

       As well as local architecture, art and colour schemes I also think that sound, particularly in retail environments, could be a great way to express global/local. Perhaps mixing the corporate sonic branding with the local musical culture?

Sam Sampson, chairman, The Brand Union

Interview with Paul Fulberg and Dan Jackson, joint managing directors, Sonicbrand. September 2002, The Brand Union, St John Street, London.

DJ   What is branding?

SS   I approach the subject from the identity aspect. The first stage of any relationship between a corporation and a consumer is that the consumer sees or hears something, recognizes it and then has an emotional reaction to it. The visual part is the corporate or brand identity.

My background was as a designer and what I have learned is that there are mechanical things that can be done to ensure that the consumer pays attention. Once these graphic devices have been used it is then up to the rest of the communication to be recognizable, legible and stimulate emotional reactions. I call that identity and it is where this industry has come from. It is the process of sending out signals. Branding is really the business of understanding their likely effect on different audiences.

DJ   Do you focus on identity because it is the only thing you can really control?

SS   Absolutely, I don't say this much in front of clients because they don't like to hear it but the consumer is completely in charge and owns the brand. Emotionally, the corporation owns nothing once it has put its product and identity out there.

The job of identity or branding is sometimes as simple as just removing the negatives from an identity. There are definitely devices in graphics and I'm sure in sound that are simply wrong for a brand – like having a spiky, dangerous-looking logo for a cuddly toy maker. If we make sure there are no negatives first, then we can go on to add some positive attributes later but, again, all we can do is identify the messages, the consumer has to receive them and that is the bit we cannot really control. I summarize the whole process as see-recognize-remember-feel.

DJ   Is there really that little control?

SS   Well, I suppose that these days we do have a little more understanding of how people receive messages and we can use stimulants such as sound or smell to accelerate the process of memorability but very often we do have little or no control. How would you control the feelings of the motorist towards a BP garage as he drives past?

DJ   You talk more about corporate identity as the process and you avoid the 'brand'. Is this a result of your heritage in the business, when CI was really all it was about?

SS   It has never just been about CI. There has always been an aspect of CI that dealt with the idea of corporate image or reputation which are really quite close to the concept of brand. I would concede however, that when I started out in 1969, most of the business focused on identification. At the time there was a kind of corporate megalomania as every large business strove to put its stamp on everything from the building to the chairman's underpants just so they could show how big and important they were.

Back then, the consumer was everything and though we recognized that there were various groups within the consumer body, they were usually treated as one. It was only quite recently that we really worked out that much of the job of identity had been to influence the financial community. That recognition sparked a real change of direction and the emphasis for CI became the emotional engineering of a brand.

Another part of this was the movement for corporate social responsibility (CSR). Again, this was really driven by a desire for corporations to identify themselves as being 'good' to the financial community. I like the FTSE For Good and what it means for the future.

PF   Changing tack slightly, there is a movement towards brand guardians being employed by corporations. At the moment they seem to be design-led. Should brand guardianship be broader and cover all marketing disciplines?

SS   Yes, definitely and I see that many of the corporations I work with have brand guardians with broad reach. I think the idea of a 'logo cop' just wouldn't be worth employing. Boots, a company I know well, has a brand guardian whose job it is to oversee all activities from a brand perspective. Whether that person has sonic branding knowledge I don't know but it seems to me they should definitely be interested.

Andrew Ingram, account planning director, Radio Advertising Bureau

Interview with Dan Jackson, joint managing director, Sonicbrand. December 2002, The Radio Advertising Bureau, Shafesbury Avenue, London.

DJ   Andrew, you and the RAB were among the first to recommend sonic branding in the UK. When and where did you first become aware of the concept?

AI   I guess, like many people, I became particularly aware of Intel at the start of the 1990s but that was after I had been involved with the launch of Direct Line in 1989, which was really my first hands-on experience of sonic branding. I was working at Davis Wilkins as the account planner when we came up with the brand's first ad campaign, which immediately became iconic, just as Intel's did a couple of years afterwards.

I remember we put the animatic of the TV ad into research with Millward Brown, who did their Link™ test on it. About 150 people were shown the ad while holding a little lever that they could use to express how much the ad interested them. When the little red telephone and the sonic came on the screen, the numbers blew off the dial. The results were very strong in testing and when the campaign launched, I'm proud to say it won an IPA [Institute of Practitioners in Advertising] effectiveness award.

Almost overnight, the phone and the sonic entered the language as an audio-visual mnemonic. It was all rather traditional in a way. Chris Wilkins, the creative director of the agency, called it an 'old-fashioned advertising gimmick'. If you think about it, he was really saying that it was a tried and tested way of generating awareness quickly and it did prove incredibly powerful.

When I joined the RAB and started thinking about radio, we started calling such things sonicbrand triggers. Capital Radio (or their sales organization MSM) had also identified this as an important area with Diarmid Moncrieff's work – I think they talked of 'sonic logos' at the time. Our first booklet on the subject was called *A Guide to Using Sonic Brand Triggers*.

DJ   Sonicbrand trigger is the RAB's term for a sonic logo?

AI   They are both a particular area of the whole sonic branding thing. In the booklet we asked some interesting people about them, how they worked and how to make them work. I particularly remember talking to Corky McGuinness, a music professor at Royal Holloway College in London. She demonstrated to me the links between music, rhythm and melody and the way our memories work. She particularly talked about how we memorize nursery rhymes during childhood.

DJ   That's a good point. We all have an innate understanding of the principles of sonics from childhood and yet there is always a need from some people for bar charts and graphs and research. It seems a little lazy to me. Sometimes I wonder why people won't think and act on their instincts – it worked for Luke Skywalker.

AI   We must have been asked 100 times for some research of a brand that owns sonic branding but has tested not using it versus using it. I don't understand why that research would ever be done. Once a brand has some strong sonic branding, it seems to me they always use it.

DJ   Have you done any research into sonics to satisfy those that want it?

AI   I have found that the people who ask about research are actually trying to prove a case in an argument between clients who want sonics and agencies who don't. I prefer not to get involved in that kind of scenario. We do, however, have some research planned through the Internet for next year.

DJ   That's good to hear. The definitive research on sonic branding has yet to be done, I hope this goes some way towards proving the case in numbers that is already understood by gut-feel. At the RAB, what do you feel makes good sonic branding?

AI   First, it has to be distinct. Second, it must be recognizable and thirdly, it must have a number of links or associations. We actually see it as a three-stage process. The distinctiveness must be designed in, and is an investment. Recognition only comes from frequency of exposure and is again an investment. The third stage, where the sonic branding becomes associated with benefits or linked with an idea is where the branding starts to pay back and can really become important.

There is an old saying in advertising that says that clients get bored of ads before consumers do. I think that is probably true with sonic branding in many cases. They take a lot of investment and the brand needs to stick by them for quite a long time before they become powerful enough to start paying back. I think some clients are already bored by the time recognition starts to build and they look for the next thing.

DJ   Do you remember how long it took from the launch of Direct Line until the sonic was recognized and linked with the visual and the benefits of the brand?

AI   The launch advertising ran for six months at the beginning of 1989. When we were approaching the end of the initial burst we started asking questions about what to do next and it was then that we realized how important the sonic and the phone had become. Of course, recognizing this, we had to maintain their presence in the next advertising campaign and it has now become a classic piece of UK ad history.

DJ   As the account planner, were you involved in recommending the sonic for Direct Line?

AI   Not really, it was led by Steve Ashman, marketing manager at the time. His thinking led the creative director Chris Wilkins to set his sights on blowing the needle off the dial on the Link test for brand recall, persuasiveness and enjoyability. He succeeded.

DJ   It has often been imitated, too. Admiral Insurance launched not long after Direct Line with their sound-alike.

AI   Yes, it was a very similar sonic and I think it muddied the waters for a while, until it was withdrawn. If they had used a different instrument or something to be more distinct then I think it could have been just as effective for them as it had been for Direct Line.

DJ   Are there any other sonics that you know have researched particularly well?

AI   Do you remember Norwich Union's use of the tune 'You Can't Get Me I'm Part of the Union'? That, I remember, raised awareness of that brand in one massive leap – way beyond anything it had ever had before. If they hadn't merged with some other institutions it would still be a very powerful brand property. Saatchi and Saatchi came up with the campaign. Adding that to their experience with British Airways, they have some pretty good credentials in sonic branding.

DJ   Do you have any thoughts on the future of sonic branding?

AI   Well, I actually think there are some interesting things going on at the moment which have to be evaluated before we talk about the future. Intel and Direct Line are the best-known sonics at the moment but I actually think they are a bit clunky – very conspicuous and obvious. They were designed to be memorable but I think that the next stage is to view sonics as a property that can contribute to a brand positioning that is more subtle and less 'in your face'.

    Delibes for British Airways, Bach for Hamlet Cigars and also Nescafé's 'Open Up' theme were all steps towards this use of sonics. I thought the Nescafé sonic was particularly good but it only ran for 18 months or so. It was a shame. Marmite, too, has great sonic branding. They use a jazz funk standard called Lowrider and it is perfect. The music itself has a love it or hate it quality. Also Go, the low-cost airline, had a great piece of music that had the perfect musical fit with the brand. It is unfortunate that the Go branding is being abandoned now that easyJet have bought them: but I am quite sure the sonic branding played an important in making them an attractive buy.

DJ   There are quite a few brands that do use sonics in a subtle way but there are still so many that do not think about why or if they could benefit from sonic branding. Why do you think that is?

AI   I think that Process has much to do with it and this goes back to my earliest thoughts on Diarmid's work. Most people know sonics work for others but they have never been told how to make them work for their brand. Brand managers must be helped with this and they need a resource they can turn to. I would guess sonic branding comes under the aegis of 'media-neutral planning', which means it probably sits outside of traditional ad agencies. I think ad agencies are reluctant to get involved with sonic branding because they feel it will be constricting. Media agencies and clients do not know anything about it so it is left up to very few people to go out and recommend this stuff.

To me, the future is to build the sophistication of sonic branding and probably reference the past by bringing back some good old-fashioned jingles. There is such an open territory right now. I think that if a brand took the leap and started really using a traditional-style jingle on commercial radio that the success would be phenomenal.

DJ   Jingles are one of my favourite subjects. They are little bits of poetry and music – works of art in my opinion.

AI   We all remember so many of them as well. They define every generation in the same way as popular music. We are trained to remember them; I know one person at the RAB, Mark Barber, who simply remembers every single jingle he has ever heard!

DJ   They work because they generate a kind of Pavlovian response where a benefit becomes linked to a sound. I know that you are a Tony Hancock fan – when you hear that theme music you know you are in for a treat.

AI   The only thing holding them back right now is the negative associated within the ad industry with the word 'jingle'. They are linked with strap-lines and girls draped over bonnets of cars – old fashioned. It is important that the terms are brought up to date to avoid this.

DJ   Back to research for a moment. At the RAB conference last month you presented the results of a large study you carried out in conjunction with Millward Brown. As I recall, the main finding was that the most popular radio commercials are those with a good mix of likeability and branding.

I know from my time at Capital Radio that the sales force leads on the concept of branding on radio. Is that a part of the RAB's agenda?

AI   We aren't leading on it but I'm sure it is a relevant argument. Unfortunately, there are not enough good case studies of radio acting alone to build a brand.

DJ   But radio does not have to act alone. The same person listening to Heart FM in the morning watches ITV in the evening. Radio as a branding medium simply has to be integrated with the rest of the communication.

AI   Yes, that makes sense. In that respect, I think that Carphone Warehouse is a good case study of branding using commercial radio. Though the bulk of their success must be attributed to the stores and the way they treat customers, radio was used in a very consistent and effective way to drive customers to the store. The media strategy at least has to be termed good branding, they were able to reach potential customers at greater frequencies and at more relevant times than TV would have allowed.

The creative strategy, using the Stereo MC's 'Connected' was a device much like Direct Line's in that it was memorable and consistent but I'm not sure how much it added to the brand positioning. I actually like what they are doing now with Ed Byrne voicing their mobile phone character. It is distinct and consistent but also adds to an emotional understanding of the brand.

Robbie Laughton, executive creative director, Wolff Olins

Interview with Paul Fulberg, joint managing director, Sonicbrand. September 2002, Wolff Olins, Kings Cross, London N1.

PF   Robbie, how would you define a brand?

RL   Brands start at the centre of a company or organization and what a brand is, is a belief. That is the most distilled definition I can give you. I have been working with brands for 20 years and each one of them had a common belief that held the company or organization together.

PF   If belief is at the centre of a brand, what are the other ingredients?

RL   My conception of brands is that they start with beliefs that are turned into ideas. These ideas then form a basis for the behaviour of the organization that in some way must create a benefit or set of benefits for the customers.

PF   That is clear enough. Some brand theory, though, says that advertising is at the centre of a brand. You have not even mentioned it. Is this consistent with the belief theory?

RL   Advertising can be a very important entry point into a brand, for a customer but it is not absolutely essential to brands. For example, some people think that the branding of Tango, the orange-flavoured soft drink, started with an ad campaign. Remember the 'You know when you've been Tango'd' strap-line? People remember that and think that the advertising was responsible for the whole reinvention of the brand.

The truth is that many customers discovered Tango as a result of seeing the advertising but many also discovered it when they saw it in the fridge in the newsagents or when their mate brought a can to school. The advertising was just one of the entry points to the brand. What was at the centre of the brand, however, was the belief of the people at Tango that their soft drink had something special about it. If they had not believed in it, they would never have even briefed an ad agency.

PF   So if advertising is just another entry point to a brand, what are the others and is there a hierarchy? Are some entry points more important than others?

RL   If we just talk about customers rather than internal audiences, the retail environment can be very important. Coke is very good at its distribution and presentation in retail is a major key to their success. Plenty of companies these days have call centres as the first point of entry. There, a phone number and a person in Glasgow wearing a headset can be the first way in to a brand.

Sometimes direct mail, the Internet, an exhibition stand or a sponsored event can be the first entry points. There is no hierarchy as such, because each entry point has to be on-brand in order to support the others.

PF   What does on-brand mean?

RL   On-brand really means two things: consistency, maintained by the central belief in the brand; what it stands for and where its ambitions lie.

I worked extensively on the development of the Orange brand and where it gained its success was down to a consistency where the product and the communication were aligned to tell the same story. Problems with brands arise when there is a misalignment of product or communications. In other words, the advertising might make a number of promises but the product does not deliver. Companies used to be able to get away with making promises they didn't keep but these days, more and more, they are being found out.

We [Wolff Olins] do a lot of work on behaviour, for all the people who work in a company. This is not to say we try and make everyone a clone, we don't. What we do is to try and explain the brand's beliefs to the staff and try to make sure that the company itself, in the way it behaves towards them, is also on-brand. In this way, any person in a call centre, when called upon to be the entry point to a brand, can be as strong a spokesperson as the managing director. This is the only way, for example, for a bank that advertises itself as being service oriented, to keep its promise.

We have to remember that keeping promises, being consistent, to staff and customers is everything because customers particularly can either make you a hero or reduce you to nothing.

PF   You mentioned Orange and it seems to be a brand that has certainly been a hero to many. It seems to have been making a few mistakes recently. When it sponsored Glastonbury, it was pilloried and had eggs thrown at its hoardings. Why do you think that happened?

RL   I don't think Orange had a right to be at Glastonbury because they were not seen to be improving the event or funding the event but were seen to be jumping on a bandwagon. They also did this with the BAFTA sponsorship though the audience reaction was less severe.

It would have been much better for them if they were actually doing something new and interesting for people rather than just slapping their logo on an existing event. Instead of sponsoring Glastonbury, they could fund other gigs. Instead of sponsoring the BAFTA awards – which I think was pointless – they could have really got behind young film-makers.

PF   A great example of actually giving something to the people is from Red Bull, the energy drink. As well as sponsorships of skateboarding events, they have actually built skate parks and ramps. This has given them real credibility within a cynical youth market.

RL   That is exactly the kind of thing I'm talking about. We helped re-launch an Israeli telco [telecom company] that had to answer the challenge of the Orange brand. Instead of just building logo awareness they tried to make the country a little bit better through a diverse range of services from portaloos at the beach to unbranded Internet cafés.

PF   The fact that the service is unbranded is a big plus. People are certainly a little tired of all the logos they see these days. Also, the free flow of information means that the people are sure to hear about the benevolent service provider in a longer-term, less intrusive way.

Back to Orange. In the light of its recent sponsorship mistakes, do you have a feeling that it has come to the end of its life cycle?

RL   Yes and no. It is certainly in need of refreshment but that is hardly surprising. I have worked with a number of telcos and I have seen that there is a brand life cycle of about five years. Some are even quicker. I remember that One2One, now T-Mobile, at one stage in its life had three different look and feel treatments in one year.

       It is brand management that gives us an insight into when a brand needs refreshing. Brand management is really all about keeping your eyes and ears open in order to find out what people think of a brand. Again, it is the customers who are most important. Talking to them constantly gives insight into the state of a brand.

PF   As a customer, I still believe in the Orange branding versus the other telcos. They just seem the most focused on providing a phone service. What has changed for Orange that needs refreshing?

RL   When Orange launched it had a unique set of values that led to its unique positioning. In a market that was complex and confusing, where Cellnet and Vodafone had loads of different tariffs and retail offers, Orange was deliberately simple, clear and optimistic. You were a consumer then and now. You remember that positioning and the consistent way in which it was communicated has had a lasting effect on you.

       What started out as a revolutionary offering, however, has been copied to such a degree that the Orange values are now hygiene values for any telcos brand. New customers, the ones that are just coming into the market, expect them as basics or they won't touch the company.

       Now O_2 and T-Mobile have copied Orange, it needs to be rethought. It needs some new belief. I think that '3' the new third generation mobile brand from Hutchison is going to shake up the market just like Orange did in the 1990s. It is going to be pretty radical, even more so than Virgin mobile.

PF   Virgin is an interesting one. Is it at the end of its life-cycle too?

RL   I don't think so but it certainly has its own problems. It has always been a David versus other brand Goliaths. Now it is a big brand itself and it is going to be attacked as such, particularly in the telecoms market. It will also suffer in that Virgin has broken a few promises, especially in its train operations. Railtrack may be the reason and Virgin will be able to blame them for a while but not forever.

       Virgin also has to overcome the fatigue associated with Branson as a front man. Every brand needs a leader but he was, perhaps, a little over-exposed for some time. It is also important for such a big brand as Virgin to be able to live without a single leader. I have respect for Stelios [Haji-Ioannou] for stepping back from easyJet and allowing it to grow without him. The skill set for maintaining and growing a mature brand are quite different from the entrepreneurial skills that put Branson and Stelios where they are.

PF   Virgin is one of the best examples of where a brand has extended itself across a number of different products and services. Do you think it is devalued because it is spread thinly?

RL   Extending a brand should always add value as long as the extensions continue to support the central belief and everyone knows their role. Orange extended their brand across the world and because the belief was and is so strong, it has had success everywhere. That is worth noting because the extensions into other countries, where the Orange brand still stands for clarity, simplicity and optimism have protected the brand at a time when, in the UK, it has come under attack.

PF   Are there any brands you particularly admire today?

RL   One that has really struck me as doing everything the right way is Innocent; the juices and smoothies manufacturer has a fantastic product with no pretence. It is clear that the people behind it all believe in it too. Interestingly, they do all their own advertising and promotions in-house. This really helps them tell their story. As a result, the brand experience is absolutely clear; everything done in the name of the brand is consistent.

I also think that Volkswagen get things spot-on these days. For me, their offering is a true cradle to grave range of products. The design is also absolutely seamless throughout the range as is the commitment to service.

PF   We have talked a lot about consistency and keeping promises but can you tell me why they are so important?

RL   It has to do with trust. It is very easy to make promises but it is far harder to stick to them, particularly in a business world dominated by the bottom line. The benefit to the brand, however, is that promises that are kept allow the brand and customer to have a relationship of trust, in just the same way as a person is only trustworthy if they keep their promises.

PF   It certainly seems like there is a lack of trust between consumers and brands these days. Nobody sets out to create an evil brand but many people have become cynical whenever they hear a promise from a company. Are we seeing that brands who become untrustworthy are the ones that suffer?

RL   Yes, but the Enron and Worldcom stories are just extreme versions of what has always gone on with brands that don't or can't keep their promises.

I remember working on the branding for the Channel 5 launch. In communications terms it was one of the most successful ever in this country. The awareness levels were up over 90%. That is in line with Coca-Cola and the Post Office, after just a few months. We raised the expectations of the audience, with the line 'Gimme Five' being adopted as a way of letting people know that the channel was for them and was going to offer them something they really wanted.

Unfortunately, the channel content itself did not live up to the expectations and even worse, many people could not receive it or got very poor reception. We had been idealistic but with hindsight it is obvious that a new channel cannot compete immediately with the far bigger budgets of the incumbents. The brand promised more than it delivered and only now is it really being re-evaluated by the audience, more than six years later. If you don't tell the truth, no matter how well intentioned, you will get found out.

PF   What is the most exciting movement in branding today?

RL   I get incredibly excited by viral marketing and the idea of peer to peer branding or brand advocacy. It is really just an extension of seeing the kid in class who has a new toy and wanting one yourself but it goes one step further.

The best viral marketing entertains first and communicates a brand second, sometimes missing out the logo altogether. What I like most about it is that my friends and I filter it before we pass it on. By doing this we show each other that we trust a brand. It is a really natural way for brands to build profile.

PF   So is advocacy the next challenge for brands?

RL   Advocacy will always be an important entry to brands, perhaps one day it will really dominate; but going forward, if a brand focuses upon consistency between product and promise, keeps its promises and builds trust then it will prosper. That remains the enduring challenge.

PF   Robbie, thanks, very interesting.

N.B. Robbie Laughton, founded and is now Creative Director of DAVE, 5 Golden Square, London W1F 9BS.

Tim Greenhill, Managing Director, Greenhill McCarron Ltd.

Interview with Paul Fulberg and Dan Jackson, joint managing directors, September 2002, Islington, London WC2.

DJ   What, in your opinion, is branding?

TG   That seems like a good place to start. Branding, despite what most of the brand consultancies have been saying for the past few years, is actually pretty simple. Branding is about creating trust, though the way it has been over-complicated has actually got in the way of trust. Branding is about creating trust through consistency between the promise and the product.

I find it remarkable that so many companies, even those that have employed the services of branding experts, have 'trust' as a brand value. It cannot be a brand value because it is quite simply what all brands have to be about. Trust and consistency are the heart of any successful brand.

In the 1980s, I put forward a theory relating to the growth of brand culture within new towns such as Milton Keynes. The theory, which I never fully tested, unfortunately, was that the populations of new towns, who were all at similar life stages, depended upon brands to give themselves identities. The trend at the time was for clothing to have the brand logo plastered as large as possible across the front. This was forming a large part of the self-expression of the population of new towns and was a cultural phenomenon that resonated with other social groups around the world.

The decline and demise of the traditional organizations such as the church, trade unions and the police, coupled with displacement from extended family, lead to insecurity in new-town society that brands helped answer.

DJ   Through consistency and trust?

TG   Yes; this was only an echo of what had gone before. The United States, where brands really took hold, is a country full of previously displaced people looking for an identity and for something in which they can believe. Brands are very important, culturally, because they provide some stability. Even fashion brands like Levis are consistent in that they are constantly changing. In many it doesn't matter what a brand does, as long as it is consistent.

DJ   It is interesting that you criticize some brand consultancies for over-complicating the subject. Is there a science to it that is worthy of detailed formulae?

TG   There is a scientific side, in that brands can be measured, though not fully described. Some brand consultancies, in their drive to value brands and put them on the balance sheet have missed the most important points.

Brands are involved, emotive and intangible. All brands live in the consumer as beliefs. Brand consultancy should only ever be about making sure the consumer maintains their belief, but there is a lot of extraneous stuff that goes on in the name of brands.

Brand management requires us to understand that people buy the same product for totally different reasons. Essentially, purchase is an emotional process that involves the individual ranking the relative importance of different attributes. For example, if I buy a Ford rather than a Mercedes, it is because I value economy of running costs above prestige. If I buy a Toyota rather than an Alfa Romeo it is because I value reliability above driving pleasure. I speak for myself but every purchase by every consumer is essentially the same process of weighing up attributes.

I think of a brand as a diamond. It is one entity but it has many different facets that themselves appear differently in different light. Thus, brands are very complicated even though the central tenet of building and maintaining trust is quite simple.

DJ   Is there a brand that you have worked with that you feel has the right approach to managing its brand?

TG   I have been involved with the marketing of BMW for over 20 years and they have been very consistent throughout that time. I think I'm right in saying that BMW's four core brand values: driving, exclusivity, performance and technology have remained unchanged.

The brand values, though, are just the start of what the brand means. I'll ask you a question. If BMW made a table, what would it look like?

DJ   Lots of carbon fibre and chrome, very modern.

TG   What about a Jaguar table?

DJ   Walnut finish and traditional styling.

TG   I agree. That is how powerful the consistency of certain brands can be. BMW and Jaguar have never built tables but we both agree what they would look like if they were on-brand. Some companies think that the words describing their brand values answer all the questions, but our conception of a BMW table is not described within their values.

DJ   Are you saying that written and verbal language are not sophisticated enough to be used as brand descriptors?

TG   Good question, but don't be misled. All forms of communication must be employed to understand a brand. Language must be backed up with pictures, sounds and as many different emotive stimuli as possible.

I worked with a client whose brand values included the word 'security'. Working alongside a project team, we came up with a large body of creative work, mainly print, that built upon the value of security as it had been explained to us; as the security of a baby in its mother's arms. The project team has the picture of a mother and baby to remind them that this is what they stood for.

When the time came to present our work to a director who had been outside the process, he rejected all of our creative work on the grounds that it had nothing to do with security. His idea of the company was that it provided security akin to a big padlock. Emotionally, a padlock and a mother and baby are quite different.

Since then, we have never relied solely upon words to describe brands unless they are backed up by other stimuli.

DJ   A simple question. Why brand?

TG   In order to differentiate.

DJ   Is differentiation the goal?

TG   Yes and brands are just about the only way that companies can differentiate their goods and services. Manufacturing and technology are so good these days that pretty much anything can be copied almost as soon as it is launched. For example, in the world of personal finance, 30 years ago, teams of actuaries would work for months developing a new pension scheme. It would give the company a competitive advantage for many months until the competition's actuaries worked out how to replicate its terms. Today, a computer can run the numbers on a pension scheme in seconds and it can be on the market via the Web minutes later.

Prices can be beaten, products can be bettered but emotions are harder to change. Also, emotional elements such as visual or sonic branding are much easier to protect, legally, than any price point or product attribute. An example of the pull of emotions in purchase decisions is provided by Coke and Pepsi. In blind taste tests, Pepsi is the preferred product of over 50% of the UK population. Despite this, Coke outsells Pepsi in this country by three to one. Distribution plays a part but the brand really gives Coke its pre-eminence.

DJ   Are there any downsides to having a brand?

TG   There can be. 'Branding' has been adopted or hijacked, depending on how you look at it, by graphic designers. In their desire to give their clients all the answers, much of the design around brands has tended to become a straitjacket. Logos, colours and fonts have been prescribed to such a degree that they start to inhibit clear communications with the customer. If inhibited, it is harder to build trust.

This is why my brand and design philosophy is based around the idea of a 'springboard'; a starting point for communications that gives the organization room to express itself while being consistent and differentiated. It is a harder solution to sell to clients, because it involves leaving a lot of thinking up to them but it is more rewarding in the long run.

Ali Johnson, creative director, Sonicbrand

Interview with Dan Jackson, joint managing director, Sonicbrand. January 2003, Sonicbrand, Chalk Farm, London NW1.

DJ   What are the most important skills for a composer working in sonic branding?

AJ   The most important element is the nurturing of a collaborative environment between the sonic creative team, strategists, and stakeholders. This allows a project to fully utilize the creative skills of the composer in a focused way that is understood and signed off by everyone involved. This is the real trick to our business and the bringing together and integration of musical, branding and media expertise is what makes Sonicbrand unique.

DJ   Is there any cross-over with other areas of musical composition?

AJ   Composing music that expresses the essence of a brand is a skill that comes from collaboration much in the same way as a composer collaborates with a film director in order to express the essence of a film scene or character. Although all composers have a strong stylistic identity, and a personal way of doing things, it is important that we listen to, and take on board, the context in which we are expressing ourselves.

DJ   I know that film music is a great passion of yours. Which composers do you think have done the most to create the common language of film music that exists today?

AJ   My earliest exposure to, and appreciation of, film music was with the films of Hitchcock and the original *Star Wars* trilogy. I think these films perhaps more than any others have shaped the broad musical understanding of audiences.

Bernard Hermann composed the scores for the Hitchcock movies and really kicked off the modern era of film score composition with his work on Orson Welles' *Citizen Kane*. Hermann had a fantastic knowledge of the expressive range of the orchestra but was also influenced by the extended harmonies and rhythms of the jazz scene in the US. These influences, coupled with an innate understanding of how to use music to enhance dramatic impact, are what made his work special. His creation of suspense and drama with his scores for the Hitchcock films is still second to none in my opinion.

The John Williams scores for the *Star Wars* trilogy and his many collaborations with Spielberg fired my imagination as a child and started my fascination with film scores. What stood out for me then, and still does, is his expansive use of the many textures of the romantic orchestra. We should, though, give credit to his orchestrators for some of this.

He developed very strong melodic elements in his scores and his use of leitmotif in his writing is excellent. Leitmotif is a compositional technique that assigns musical themes to represent characters, locations or ideas. Just watch the original *Star Wars* and you'll hear that every time Darth Vader or the Death Star are shown, the same themes are played. It is not particularly subtle but it is very effective. Williams has created so many wonderful themes that you can listen to any film he has worked on and hear at least one great example.

To cap it all, Williams has scored seven of the top 20 box-office movies ever. This must make him the most influential in spreading a common musical language around the world.

DJ   Are there any other well known scores that you feel have taken the genre of film music on to a level beyond the kind of 'classic' approach of Hermann and Williams?

AJ   Personally, I am a big fan of the Dave Grusin score for *The Firm*, starring Tom Cruise. He takes the jazz influence to an extreme by using jazz piano as the main instrument throughout the score. Thomas Newman's score to *American*

Beauty is another of my favourites. I particularly like the way he combines ethnic percussion, marimba, guitars and sound effects with the more standard tools of synthesizer, strings and piano. The sound he creates from this ensemble is fresh and unique while still fulfilling the dramatic requirements of a film score. Similarly, many Danny Elfman scores (*Men in Black*, *Batman*) have great quirkiness of melody and orchestration that comes from his blend of orchestra and electronic sounds.

DJ   All the composers you name have come up with some very different musical styles for the films they work on. Do they all have different ways of approaching a brief or are there some universal approaches to scoring?

AJ   Obviously, every artist works in his or her own way but the questions that have to be asked and answered at the point of creation are pretty similar in most cases. Composers, together with the directors with whom they collaborate, have to make choices regarding melody, harmony, rhythm and instrumentation. In branding terms composers essentially create a set of creative guidelines for every project that they work on that encapsulate particular creative choices. They will, of course, change and elaborate as they go along but there has to be some idea of how each of these variables will be used throughout a movie. In that way, the entire score holds together as a piece in its own right. If the overall creative approach was changed scene by scene, there would be no sense of continuity.

I guess this is one of the main areas where the skills and creative approaches of a film and sonic branding composer come together. The guidelines we create at the end of the creative learning stage of the sonic branding process are essentially the same guidelines that a film composer creates after viewing the movie a few times and liaising with the director.

DJ   What are the unique challenges of sonic branding? For example, what is different about creating a sonic logo rather than a longer piece of music?

AJ   The composition of successful sonic logos, as opposed to jingles and stings that are not coming from the brand language, involves the above skills as well as practice. These executions require the compression of a melodic idea and orchestration into a short time while maintaining a strong sense of memorability, flexibility and musical depth to allow expansion and the composition of related pieces of music. This is not always as easy as writing a longer piece of music!

DJ   How do you feel the world of branding can further take advantage of expression through music and sound?

AJ   As branding becomes a more holistic affair with agencies becoming involved in the development of the strategy and ethos of a business for both internal and external audiences, the potential for the use of music becomes far greater.

At the core of a brand exists a belief which has inherent emotion attached to it. This can form the basis for the development of a musical expression and, as a result of the properties of music and its ability to stimulate emotion, can become a key vehicle in the expression of the core belief itself.

The internal cultures of businesses are becoming more important and staff are being engaged throughout a company both in the environment that they work in and in structured staff development and interactive workshops, for example.

Music and sound design has an important role to play in creating the right kinds of internal environments and can be extremely useful in supporting workshops that often rely on creating their own unique interactive environments. The work that we have done in this area has proved extremely effective. Audiences can respond and relate very quickly to audio stimulus and, in many situations, more effectively than visual stimulus alone.

Sound and acoustic design is becoming an integral part of office architecture and has an important place in the processes of sonic branding. These internal touchpoints should form part of the sonic branding brief and therefore sit along-side the development process for external touchpoints with the work for each respective audience informing the other.

Glossary

The subject of sonic branding involves a number of definitions that will help ensure that you understand what we are on about in this book. I want you to have access to all you need to create or manage sonic branding projects and to this end, I have to remove as much ambiguity and subjectivity as I can from my language, which means defining the key terms used in this book.

Brand: An idea, stemming from belief, that through its consistent identity, experience and the positive emotional investment (PEI) of stakeholders, creates sustainable benefits.

Brand experience: The totality of all the consistent touchpoints of a brand.

Brand score: The core expression of a brand's sonic identity.

Branding: The creation and consistent management of distinct, memorable, flexible and honest brand identity and experience.

Jingle: A rhyming, usually musical, brand mnemonic.

Sonic branding: The creation and consistent management of distinct, memorable, flexible and honest brand identity and experience, in sound.

Sonic layering: Creative development process, matching brand values to musical layers.

Sonic logo™: The symbol of a brand in sound. Usually less than 20 seconds in length.

Speechfonts™: Vocal classification system matching brand values to vocal qualities.

Stakeholders: All the people involved with a brand at all levels.

Touchpoints: The channels through which a brand communicates with its stakeholders.

References

Preface

1. P. Stephenson, *Billy* (HarperCollins Entertainment, 2001), p. 290.
2. P.F. Drucker, *Post Capitalist Society* (Harper Business, 1994), p. 10.
3. N. Klein, *No Logo* (Flamingo, 2001), p. 5.

Chapter 1

1. C. Dowdy, 'Sonic Mnemonic', *Financial Times: Creative Business* (30 January 2000), p. 7.

Chapter 2

1. Western Electrician.

Chapter 3

1. Interview with Steven Spielberg in Channel 4's *100 Greatest Films 2002*.
2. Drawn in part from R. Davis, *Complete Guide to Film Scoring* (Berklee Press, 1999), pp. 39–45.

Chapter 4

1. Website of the Radio Advertising Bureau, UK, **www.rab.co.uk**.

Chapter 5

1. E. Gurney, *The Power of Sound* (Smith, Elder, 1880), p. 119.
2. M. Clynes, *Music, Mind and Brain: The Neuropsychology of Music* (Plenum, 1982), pp. 47–82.

Chapter 6

1. T. White, 'A Man Out Of Time Beats The Clock', *Musician*, no. 60 (October 1983), p. 52.
2. Drawn in part from R. Brunelle, 'The Art Of Sound Effects', *Experimental Musical Instruments*, vol. 12 no. 1 and vol. 12 no. 2 (1996).
3. 'A Man out of time beats the clock', *Musician Magazine*, no. 60 (Oct 1983), p. 52.
4. H.S. Thompson, *Generation of the Swine: Tales of Shame and Degradation in the 80s* (Summit Books, 1988), p. 43.

Chapter 7

1. *New Oxford Dictionary of English.*
2. Peter Montoya with Tim Vandehey *The Personal Branding Phenomenon* (Personal Branding Press, 2002).

Chapter 8

1. Committee on Definitions of the American Marketing Association, *Marketing Definitions* (AMA, 1960).
2. R. Berry, *Jung* (Hodder & Stoughton, 2001), p. 42.
3. Herbert Hoover's Speech at the US Department of Commerce conference on radio telephony (27 February–2 March 1922).
4. R. Clifton and E. Maughn, *The Future of Brands* (Palgrave Macmillan, 2000), p. vii.

Chapter 9

1. B. Schmitt and A. Simonson, *Marketing Aesthetics* (The Free Press, 1997), p. 65.
2. E. Schlosser, *Fast Food Nation* (Penguin, 2001), p. 50.

Chapter 10

1. *New Oxford Dictionary of English.*
2. L. Armstrong, 'If You've Got It, Don't Flaunt It', *The Times T2* (11 October 2002) pp. 4–5.
3. D. Jackson and P. Fulberg's interview with Tim Greenhill, September 2002.
4. P. Fulberg's interview with Robbie Laughton, September 2002.

Chapter 11

1. Patrick Hanks, *New Oxford Thesaurus of English* (Oxford University Press, 2000).
2. M. Robinson, *Sunday Times 100 Greatest TV Ads* (HarperCollins, 2000).

Chapter 12

1. M. Rokeach, *The Nature of Human Values* (The Free Press, 1972), p. 5.

Chapter 13

1. B. Schmitt and A. Simonson, *Marketing Aesthetics* (The Free Press, 1997), p. 3.

Chapter 18

1. D. Jackson and P. Fulberg's interview with Phil Horton (August 2002).
2. D. Jackson and P. Fulberg's interview with David Magliano (July 2002).
3. G. Marshall, **www.geofftech.co.uk**.

Chapter 23

1. Quoted in Harley-Davidson press release, 20 June 2000.

Summary

1. Aristotle, *Politics* 8. 1340a-b: cf Plato *Laws* 2. 665–70 BC.

Recommended further reading

Aaker, D.A. *Building Strong Brands* (Free Press Business, 2002).

Abrams, B. 'Music, Cancer, and Immunity', *Clinical Journal of Oncology Nursing Integrated Care*, vol. 5, no. 5 (September–October 2001).

Beh, H.C. and Hirst, R. 'Performance on Driving-Related Tasks During Music', *Ergonomics*, vol. 42, no. 8 (1999), pp. 1087–98.

Bruner, G.C. 'Music, Mood and Marketing', *Journal of Marketing* (October 1990), pp. 94–104.

Budd, M. *Music and the Emotions* (Routledge & Kegan Paul, 1985).

Davis, R. *Complete Guide to Film Scoring* (Berklee Press, 1999).

de Chernatony, L. *From Brand Vision to Brand Evaluation* (Butterworth Heinemann, 2001).

Dube, L., Chebat, J.C. and Morin, S. 'The Effects of Background Music on Consumers' Desire to Affiliate in Buyer Seller Interactions', *Psychology and Marketing*, vol. 12, no. 4 (1995), pp. 305–19.

Fairclough, N. *New Labour, New Language* (Routledge, 2000).

Garfield, L.M. *Sound Medicine* (Celestial Arts, 1987).

Gedulf, H.M. *The Birth of the Talkies From Edison to Jolson* (Indiana University Press, 1975).

Hallam, S. and Katsarou, G. *The Effects of Listening to Background Music on Children's Altruistic Behaviour and Success in Memorising Text*, Paper presented at the conference of the British Educational Research Association Belfast (27–30 August 1998).

Hargreaves, D.J. and North A.C. *The Social Psychology of Music* (Oxford University Press, 1997).

Hopkins, A.A. *Magic, Stage Illusions and Trick Photography* (Dover Publications, 1990).

Jorgenson, J. *Encyclopaedia of Consumer Brand: Durable Goods* (St James' Press, 1994).

Jung, C. *Man and His Symbols* (Aldus Books, 1964).

Klapholz, J. 'Fantasia: Innovations in Sound', *Journal of the Audio Engineering Society*, vol. 39, no 1–2 (1991), pp. 66–70.

Klein, N. *No Logo* (Flamingo, 2001).

Landry, R.J. *This Fascinating Radio Business* (Bobbs-Merrill Co., 1946).

MacDonald J.F. *Don't Touch That Dial! Radio Programming in American Life from 1920 to 1960* (Nelson-Hall, 1982).

McCallion, M. *The Voice Book* (Faber & Faber, 1988).

Milliman, R.E. 'The Influence of Background Music on the Behaviour of Restaurant Patrons', *Journal of Consumer Research*, no. 13 (1986), pp. 286–9.

Milliman, R.E. 'Using Background Music to Affect the Behaviour of Supermarket Shoppers', *Journal of Marketing*, no. 46 (1982), pp. 86–91.

Montoya, P. and Vandehay, T. *The Brand Called You* (self-published, 1999).

Mott, R. *Sound Effects: Radio, TV and Film* (Focal Press, 1990).

Newman, R.I., Hunt, D.I. and Rhodes, F. 'The Effects of Music on Employee Attitude and Productivity in a Skateboard Factory', *Journal of Applied Psychology*, vol. 50, no. 6 (1996), pp. 493–6.

North, A.C., Hargreaves, D.J. and MacKenzie, L.C. 'Music and Morale in the Workplace', *Report for the Performing Right Society* (2000).

North, A.C. and MacKenzie, L.C. 'Musical Tempo, Productivity and Morale', *Report for the Performing Right Society* (2000).

Olson, G.D. 'The Sounds of Silence: Functions and Use of Silence in Television Advertising', *Journal of Advertising Research*, no. 34 (1994), pp. 89–95.

Schmitt, B. and Simonson, A. *Marketing Aesthetics* (The Free Press, 1997).

Sloboda, J. 'Music Structure and Emotional Response: Some Empirical Findings', *Psychology of Music*, vol. 19, no. 2 (1995), pp. 110–20.

Smulyan, S. *Selling Radio: The Commercialization of Radio Broadcasting, 1920–34* (Smithsonian Institution, 1994).

Storr, A. *Music and The Mind* (HarperCollins, 1997).

West M.J. and King A.P. 'Mozart's Starling', *American Scientist*, no. 78 (1990), p. 106.

Wishart, T. *On Sonic Art* (Harewood Academic Publishers, 1996).

Young-Witzel, G. and Witzel, M.K. *Soda Pop!* (Raincoast Books and Coca-Cola Company, 1998).

Web resources

www.brandchannel.com
www.inta.org
www.Intel.com
www.Landor.com
www.nationalgeographic.com
www.rab.co.uk
www.rab.com
www.thepowerofmusic.co.uk

Index

CPI Antony Rowe
Chippenham, UK
2017-06-17 03:25